LIVING OUR FUTURE:
FRANCIS OF ASSISI AND THE CHURCH TOMORROW

Mario von Galli S.J.

Living our Future: Francis of Assisi and the Church Tomorrow

With Color Photos by Dennis Stock

Translated by
Maureen Sullivan and John Drury

FRANCISCAN HERALD PRESS
1434 WEST 51st STREET • CHICAGO, 60609

Living Our Future: Francis of Assisi and the Church Tomorrow, by Mario von Galli S. J., with color photos by Dennis Stock, translated by Maureen Sullivan and John Drury from the German, *Gelebte Zukunft: Franz von Assisi,* originally published in 1970 by Verlag C. J. Bucher, Luzern und Frankfurt/M.

Library of Congress Catalog Card Number: 72-77444.

© 1972, by Franciscan Herald Press, 1434 West 51st St., Chicago, Ill. 60609. ISBN: 8199-0439-2.

Nihil Obstat:
 Mark Hegener O.F.M.
 Censor Deputatus

Imprimatur:
 Rt. Rev. Msgr. Francis W. Byrne
 Vicar General, Archdiocese of Chicago

May 15, 1972.

"The Nihil Obstat and Imprimatur are official declarations that a book or pamphlet is free of doctrinal or moral error. No indication is contained therein that those who have granted the Nihil Obstat and Imprimatur agree with the contents, opinions, or statements expressed."

Printed 1972 in Switzerland by C. J. Bucher AG, Luzern.

Contents

1. Why I Wrote this Book 7

2. His Father's Child 21

3. Living the Gospel 49

4. Poverty: The Future of the Church 83

5. Francis, the Revolutionary 159

6. Noblesse 201

7. Chronology 229

8. Bibliography 236

1. Why I Wrote this Book

Not long ago a woman journalist who had worked as a reporter at the Council asked me what I was doing at the moment. I told her that I was completely absorbed in writing a book about Francis of Assisi. "Oh, nothing interesting there," was her disappointed reply. She is a Catholic of the "progressive" sort. A book about Francis: that could only be a pious work, one that smacked of the "edification" that people do not welcome today. At best it would be an historical study, but even that would be oriented toward the past, not at all topical.

So how did the idea of writing a book about Francis of Assisi come to me? It grew – as is so often true – out of a series of accidental circumstances. First of all, Dennis Stock's photographs of the Umbrian landscape were there before me, such peerless reproductions they almost make you believe you can hear the clear voice of the Poverello of Assisi. He was the Provençal minstrel of these woods and fields and streams; of these gnarled, tapering olive trees and cypresses and thistles; of these oxen, sheep, and doves. Their voices are heard through the mouth of this man who was so intertwined with his native home that he became one with it – even though he began a worldwide movement which, as he wished, was to encompass all the countries of Europe and even the Orient. This was the place he chose to be the midpoint, the pulsing heart as it were. From it blood would be pumped through the arteries. To it blood would return for revitalization after its wearisome journey.

So the pictures were the occasion and also the starting point of this book. I saw them and they appealed to me. But I had not thought then of writing a book. Others urged me to do it. I protested that I did not know more about the saint than any average

Picture page 9:
"If God should someday deign to reveal the Order of the future to His Church ... it will surely bear the stamp of Francis' soul and spirit."

PETER LIPPERT S.J.

"The saintly Francis wandered through town and countryside.
The power of his words, not taught to him by any man,
evoked the wonder of educated men as well.
And many rushed to see and hear him
as if he had come from a different century."

LEGEND OF THE THREE COMPANIONS

Fresco by Benozzo Gozzoli (1420–1497)
in the Galleria Nazionale dell' Umbria, Perugia.

Picture pages 10–11:
The Legend of the Three Companions begins thus:
"Just as the rising sun floods and fructifies the world
with gleaming rays of light,
so Francis broke in upon the world
like a new ray of light.
It was the dawning of spring in the world."

Picture page 12:
When Francis broke with his father, he headed for a friend in Gubbio. Clad only in an old cloak, which the Bishop had given him and on which he had chalked a white cross, he moved through countryside like this. Bandits fell upon him and asked him who he was. He replied: "I am the herald of the great king, but what is that to you?" They dumped him into a ditch, which still bore traces of snow even though it was April, and said: "Lie there, peasant who would play the role of herald." Then they took off. Francis got up and continued on his way to Gubbio.

Catholic. I pointed out that there were scores of learned Franciscans (friars, nuns, priests, etc.) who by their vocation were better acquainted with their founding father than I, a Jesuit. I referred to the vast literature that exists on Francis. Just to survey it takes time. But no one listened to my objections. They didn't want a scholarly book. They wanted e book of spontaneous impressions such as a man of today might be able to offer.

Was I supposed to have a soul somehow akin to that of Francis? Those who plied me openly hinted in that direction. Whether they were right about that, I cannot decide. But in any case, I can't deny that although I began the study of Francis of Assisi half-heartedly, I proceeded to fall under his spell.

I must admit that I carried out my reading as unsystematically as you can imagine. First I read Gilbert Chesterton's little book about the saint. I love Chesterton. His mind and spirit bore an original stamp. He holds to his own judgment, and he is not at all inclined to give the customary edifying portrait that I dread so much in literature on the saints. So I read Chesterton, and I was richly rewarded. His Francis is certainly not a stereotype! But what in his presentation is really Francis, and what is the poetic creation of Chesterton? And what about the fascinating but controversial idea posed in the second chapter? There he describes the awakening of the world in the twelfth and thirteenth centuries as the end of the penitential period which necessarily followed paganism: "The purge of paganism is complete at last" (Gilbert Chesterton, *St. Francis of Assisi,* New York: Doubleday Image Book, 1957, p. 36). At that moment "a figure appeared silently and suddenly on a little hill above the city, dark against the fading darkness. For it was the end of a long and stern night, a night of vigil, not unvisited by stars. He stood with his hands lifted, as in so many statues and pictures, and about him was a burst of birds singing; and behind him was the break of day" *(Ibid.,* pp. 36–37).

Even if that holds true for the High Middle Ages, what significance does this figure still have for us today? At the end of his fine monograph on Francis of Assisi (1958) Ivan Gobry gave a surprising view of the impact of the saint in today's Non-

Catholic world. There he says that the "heretic" Renan called Francis "the only perfect Christian since Jesus," and that Gandhi praised him as one of the greatest wise men of the world. There are also testimonials from Rainer Maria Rilke and Max Picard. And Gobry maintains that there are clear "points of contact" between the spirit of St. Francis and the following: the theandry of a Solovyev and Berdyaev, the personalism of Gabriel Marcel and Emmanuel Mounier, and Teilhard de Chardin's idea of the progressive upward transformation of creation. Here in his view it is evident that Francis reaches beyond the Middle Ages. He even goes so far as to attribute to the Franciscan spirit the fact that already in the thirteenth century, "in opposition to the accepted methods," the Franciscan Roger Bacon became a forerunner of experimental science.

I could go no further. I had to go back to the sources. First I found the anthology edited by Otto Karrer, *Franz von Assisi: Legenden und Laudes* (1951). There I actually had all the essentials together. On the one hand it contained the old sources: the so-called *Legend of the Three Companions* (Ceprano), the oldest biography by Thomas of Celano, the legend of young Clare, the saintly portrait of St. Francis by the great Bonaventure, the *Fioretti,* the songs of praise by the saint, and his *Testament.* And on the other hand it had critical introductions and notes for all these pieces. I was delighted as I read it because I was now seeing a saint from the inside. I don't believe there is another saint whose thoughts and feelings, loving and suffering, one is permitted to enter into in this way. Critical distance from the standpoint of history was provided by the introduction and commentary of the editor, for Karrer is a recognized historian. But while the keen analyst is almost always in control of his material in his other writings, here the soul of a great man, a saint, takes over and carries him beyond himself.

Was I on the right track? The remarks of a young Capuchin convinced me that I was. I asked him what actually fed his spiritual life as a Franciscan, as a follower of Francis. Was it biographies, modern critical studies, books about Franciscan spirituality?

He replied, "Certainly, there are many studies of all sorts that are very valuable: the biography of Father Cuthbert (Wildlöcher), the studies of Laurentius Casutt and Hilarin Felder."

"A member of the Third Order named Jörgensen's biography to me as the best book," I said. "And a Protestant referred me to the life of the Calvinist minister and Franciscan scholar, Paul Sabatier – you can't very well pass that up even today. Another showed me the voluminous work of Henry Thode, which describes the spreading influence of Francis at the start of Renaissance art. Or maybe I should go more deeply into the source material edited by the German Franciscans?"

My young Capuchin was silent for a while. Then he said, "Personally I live by Karrer's anthology. Further research – and it is not at an end by a long shot – will shed light on the scholarly study of many important questions and details, such as the four distinct rules. Maybe you know how much is unclear there: whose influence plays a part, why the one rule was "lost" or permanently "misplaced" by Brother Elias, and so forth. But for laying hold of the Franciscan spirit, all that is of secondary importance after all."

I believe the young Capuchin was right. To be sure, I have read Casutt, Felder, Jörgensen, Cuthbert (Wildlöcher), Thode. In each I discovered new details which rounded out my picture. But Karrer's anthology remained for me the center around which everything clustered. I also looked into the modern presentations and analyses, such as those of Romano Guardini and Walter Nigg, and even the novel *Saint Francis* by Nikos Kazantzakis. They all attest that Francis has not vanished along with the world picture of the Middle Ages. Indeed he has not even faded. And that is truly amazing. That is the thing which attracts me.

How is it that in our day, long before ecumenism became the rage among the Christian confessions, and long before a deep desire for ecumenical encounter found expression in the Protestant Ecumenical Council at Geneva and confirmation on the Catholic side in Vatican II, the figure of Francis of Assisi has exerted a fascination of its own upon everyone? How is it that in our era of science – the "scientific age" we like to call it – this wholly unscientific man, who by many is even called an enemy of science, nevertheless appears as an ideal? How can it be that today when we only too gladly pride ourselves on an empty and false maturity, a man addicted to childlike play, to actions which seem even downright *childish,* appeals to us? How account for the fact that although we live in an age in which everything is planned (and whether we like it or not, must be planned), we are not seeking the "man of the future" in Orders which look back to founders whose chief traits are planning and organizing, but on the contrary, in the Franciscan mentality and spirit?

I will cite here a witness who is completely beyond suspicion, the Jesuit Peter Lippert:

"The organizational principle which leads from Benedict through Dominic and Ignatius to the newer communities seems to have practically exhausted its inner possibilities. That, of course, does not mean that it could ever become superfluous or replaceable. But the fundamental newness which is precisely the thing being sought today by countless souls and in countless attempts at innovation, is to be found only along a completely different line: along the line of the original ideal of Francis. In other words: in the direction of a freely chosen life style and freely chosen bonds of love; in the direction of a life that operates through spontaneous initiative of the self rather than through great constructs of the will; in the direction of a truly living and individual personality shaped by its own inner laws and standards. If God should someday deign to reveal the Order of the future to His Church, the Order so longingly sought by many of our best people, it will surely bear the stamp of Francis' soul and spirit."

Lippert wrote that in *Stimmen der Zeit* in 1927. In the meantime much has happened, even in the spiritual realm; yet his words are still to the point today.

I admit that much seems to contradict this, but we cannot let appearances deceive us. Maybe the Little Brothers of Charles de Foucauld are closer to the "original ideal of Francis" than the present-day organizations of the Franciscan family. To the modern temperament the very name "Little Brothers" accords much better with what Francis meant than the now incomprehensible term "Friars Minor." And what is more, the manner of living, the activities, and even the clothing of the Little Brothers are more strongly suggestive of Francis than that of the Franciscans. That is also true of their distinctive way of linking the eremitical life with active apostolic work, and of the high value they place upon the simple witness of their lives in preference to preaching.

But I prefer not to pursue this line further. I do not care to offend my beloved Franciscans, who could scarcely become other than they have been constrained to become within their own stream in history. Nor do I want to rob the Little Brothers of their Charles de Foucauld, who certainly understood the Moslems better than Francis of Assisi. But still the strange parallels exist – and perhaps the Little Brothers of Charles de Foucauld had to be in order that the branches of the Franciscan family would not have to be painfully sundered once again. I mention the example of the Little Brothers only so people cannot say it is abstract speculation or backwards-looking romanticism to say that Francis still lives today.

So what does this book propose to be? A new biography? Definitely not. An account of the latest research? That even less! A new interpretation of the original ideal of Francis? Not even that. A polemic against the watering down of the original spirit? An *apologia* for the slandered, confined, persecuted, and abused Spirituals *contra* the popes and Conventuals? All that has already been written up and settled. The faults that actually have occurred in that regard are today openly admitted by the Franciscan family itself – and that is something purely Franciscan; no other order would do it so candidly. What then does this book propose to do? It proposes simply to offer a few ideas, drawn from Francis' life, about why he is today a figure pointing toward the future.

In so doing I realize that not everyone who is enthusiastic about Francis is really acquainted with him. The name Francis reminds many people only of pretty little flowers, lambs, and well-behaved birds. They don't know the incredible toughness of his passionate love of poverty. Others, who studied him more closely, have sought to present him as an anti-Catholic. This is wholly unjustified, even though he represents a truly Christian desire for reform, espoused by reformers in his own and later times, which all too often was driven from its rightful place. Still others believe that they can interpret him purely in psychoanalytic terms. Such apparent or only half-right interpretations deserve mention at best on the fringes.

It is something else which concerns us here. Namely, our future, which we would like to measure against Francis as he really was. Certainly he was a man of his time, and much in him was conditioned by that time. It could not be otherwise. Still a timeless element came to light in his time-bound figure, became clear and tangible as never before. That can be said of every saint of course. But it cannot be said of them all that their peculiar timelessness is relevant precisely for our own age. But with Francis this seems to be true. So more than the others he is a guide to the future for us. Since the days of John XXIII, Pope and Council have been urging us to interpret the signs of the time. The unexpected and surprising thing to me was that the longer I studied Francis of Assisi, the more that study helped me to read the signs of the time. Although our critical juncture in history is not the same as that faced seven hundred years ago, the same figure stands "on a little hill above the city, dark against the fading darkness." He stands with raised hands, and around him the songs of birds echo, and behind him is the dawn. That is why I have tried to write this book.

2. His Father's Child

I must begin by tearing down some cherished notions. Many people suppose St. Francis of Assisi to be a simple, transparent character about whom there is nothing problematical. I also held this view. But the more I tried to get inside the life of this man, the more strongly I felt myself pulled asunder by nearly insupportable contradictions, by tensions I could no longer resolve. In this process the saint grew greater, not smaller, in my eyes. For where I in all likelihood would go to pieces, he held together and did not shatter. It was only later I discovered that many authors had made this observation.

There is, for instance, the disconcerting contrast between the legends and the rules. Otto Karrer completely omitted the rules of all three orders because they would be out of place in a "literary anthology." Joseph Bernhart, whose book *(Franz von Assisi: Leben und Wort,* 1947) is one of the profound works about the saint, concludes in resignation: "When we compare the stories to his own writings in which practically all we see is the lawgiver laying down rules and the master of prayer teaching people to pray, we begin to wonder whether both involve the same person. Is the man of the stories the man of the written work?"

Now this contrast may be clarified somewhat by external factors; other people were involved in the composition of the rules, and, in general, writing was not the merchant's son's line. But we are still left with internal inconsistencies which obviously go much deeper. On one hand we have the joyful brother who always has a song on his lips, who urges his followers never to give way to depression because the devil fears nothing more than a cheerful man. But over against him stands a person completely crushed by the passion and death of Christ – and this is Francis too. And what is strangest of all, the periods of melancholy and the times of exaltation do not come upon the heels of one another, but are tightly interwoven. We come upon the young convert going through the forest sobbing loudly because they nailed our Lord to the cross, even as he strides over the hill land of Umbria singing troubadour songs. And his exultant "Canticle of the Sun," which has filled the whole world with joy, was composed in that miserable hovel where the rats ran over his broken body at night, when he had become completely blind and grief over the brothers who were wrecking his work had made him interiorly, and even in his outward appearance, like one crucified. No one has been able to explain this contrast.

Or take another. Francis was certainly a humble man, ready to respect anyone more highly than himself. He made a conscious effort not to seem other than he really was. To us his public professions of self-knowledge often seem grotesque. Once as he went begging through his hometown he passed a house in which the friends of his carousing days were gathered. He was ashamed to go in there, so he went on by. But immediately he was sorry. He turned around, went back to the group of friends, and acknowledged his false shame before them all. There are many such stories. "Like the others who have left the world following my example, you take me for a holy man. But I must before God and you confess...." And his "transgression" followed: that he took some meat broth during a sickness, or something similar.

His loyalty to Church authorities is nothing short of staggering. He does not wish to preach anywhere without the permission of the priest, even if the priest is a negligent and uneducated man. He goes with his first twelve companions to the Pope to have him authorize their community. That was in the year 1210 [1209 is the commonly accepted date] – when such ecclesiastical authorization was still not even prescribed.

But at the same time Francis is marked by a self-assurance that causes no less astonishment. Even before his conversion, when he was a prisoner of the Perugians, he announced with certainty: "One day the whole world will honor me." And after his conversion this self-assurance even intensified. When it came to maintaining the purity of his ideal of poverty, he unhesitatingly opposed the Bishop of Assisi, even the Pope, and his friend Cardinal Ugolino – whom he publicly exposed before all the brothers without being at all ashamed. In *Speculum Perfectionis* Brother Leo relates that when the Cardinal advised greater leniency, "Francis did not answer, but took him by the hand and led him to the general assembly of the brothers." Trembling with emotion, Francis said:

"My brothers, my brothers! The Lord has called me to the way of simplicity and humility. He has truly shown me this way for everyone who believes me and chooses to follow me. For that reason I do not want you speaking to me of anyone's monastic rule, be it St. Benedict's, St. Augustine's, or St. Bernard's. You should advise me of no other way and form of life than that which the Lord has shown and offered *me*. The Lord told *me* to be a fool for this world in *my own* way. He chose to show us no other pathway than the pathway of *this* 'knowledge.' By *your* knowledge and wisdom, however, God will destroy you. And I confidently await the stewards and emissaries of the Lord, through which he will chastise you. Then some day, to your humiliation, and whether you want to or not, you will return to your calling!"

That probably occurred on Pentecost in 1222, before 5,000 friars. The Cardinal was "deeply shocked and said nothing more. But all the friars were very much afraid." There is no denying that the self-assurance which broke through here is no less astonishing than the exaggerations and excesses of his practices of humility. Indeed it is even frightening. And this apodictic way of presenting his position is not a rarity with Francis!

I could cite further characteristics. For instance, there is his liberality, the like of which is not to be found in the greatest ruler. But right alongside it stands a downright embarrassing pettiness in the makeup of certain individual prescriptions, which seem ridiculous to us. But I will not continue with more examples. Those already mentioned are enough to show that all attempts to label St. Francis with a word are doomed from the start. I cannot agree at all with Heinrich Federer, who characterizes him as "harmony in person." Oh, no! At times that might seem true. But then the abysses open up and we are left shuddering.

So all the epithets fit – and yet, none of them fit. He is "God's knight" (Casutt), the "troubadour" (Jörgensen), the "most unaffected of the saints" (Guardini). He is "the noble soul" (Bernhart), "the obedient one" (Schneider), "the Christ-event replayed" (Sabatier). One can say, "Childlikeness is the most original trait of this most appealing of all the saints" (Schultz). Or one can call him simply "*il poverello,*" the little poor man, as his contemporaries called him. I would say that each of these epithets has its justification. Each definitely catches an essential feature. But if a person focuses on that one alone, he will not capture the essence of the saint at all. He was certainly a gallant person through and through, and the ideal of King Arthur's Round Table stamped the relationship of Francis to his companions, and indeed the whole order since, right down to our own time. But in spite of that, Francis is not to be compared, for example, with Ignatius of Loyola, who also bore the stamp of gallantry and knighthood.

All that should be mentioned first, so that what follows will not be misunderstood. This chapter is entitled "His Father's Child." It is concerned with the childlikeness of Francis of Assisi. But it does not claim that this term exhausts his personality or even that it is his most striking trait. It may be that many people are strongly attracted by this manner of the saint. It makes him *simpatico.* It suffuses his whole being. He is not at all coolly calculating – becoming the perfect Christian through calculation. He is not a "well-tempered clavichord." He is not a supple instrument of intellect and will thanks to training and self-control. He is not that kind of man who is always amiable and a trifle unctuous, whose presence oppresses us and makes us silently wish he would curse now and then. To be sure – and I fully realize it – God led the Poverello along the pathway of heroic self-denial. We need only recall the leper on the road whose hand he kissed, his nursing of the incurably sick, his nausea and aversion to the morsels of food he obtained by begging. But none of that was learned from a textbook. Far from it. Underlying it was the statement of the Lord which he had taken to heart, "Francis, I will show you that there is sweetness in bitter things." And underlying it was his wholly spontaneous belief, indeed even his childlike curiosity and hunger, about entering a new realm, his longing to experience the Lord himself along pathways that call for audacity and courage. Self-conquest was not the goal. His activity was governed by a hunger to experience God in his life.

When I speak of "child" here, I am thinking of the gospel. It is against that standard that I would like to measure Francis of Assisi and our own time. I am not so much concerned with the child Jesus, although I know what role devotion to the child Jesus has played in the course of centuries – not only in the distorted version of pious institutes which sought to glorify a certain infantilism and psychic underdevelopment, but also in a more serious movement which includes such names as Berulle, Fésselon, Francis de Sales, Tauler, Ruysbroeck, and which ranges from the almost manly St. Theresa of Avila to the unfortunately named "little" Therese of Lisieux.

Behind all of it stand three sayings of Christ, sayings which in a startling way declare that the attitude of a child is the inescapable condition for entrance into the kingdom of heaven.

The first of these (Mk. 10,13–16; Lk. 18,15–17) has to do with it the way a child simply accepts something, without any have to listen to the message and let themselves be saturated with it the way a child simply accepts something, without any stipulations or conditions. The point of comparison should be noted carefully. It is not simply that "the child" in his innocence or daintiness, for example, is being set before us as a model. "Such a charming child," say his relatives and friends. Christ is not bidding us to be charming children. Neither is he bidding us to be "innocent," that is, as inexperienced, inept, and ignorant as children. The statement often made today that Christians have a duty to use their reason does not contradict Christ's condition for entrance into the kingdom. For he is surely referring to the child's complete dependence and consequent need of help. The parallel to the first beatitude is striking: "Blessed are the poor in spirit, for theirs is the kingdom of heaven" (Mt. 5,3). In these passages the lowly person in the Old Testament sense is being praised anew under the image of the child. The vocabulary has changed, but not the meaning. The most one can say is that in the new image openness to the gift has become even clearer and there is a definite allusion to the Father in heaven.

The background of this first saying is the disciples' attempt to keep the children away from Jesus. Our Lord was not pleased by it: "Let the children come to me, do not hinder them; for to such belongs the kingdom of God" (Mk. 10,14). The background of our second passage is different. The disciples ask Jesus who will be the greatest in the kingdom of heaven. His angry reply is, "Truly, I say to you, unless you turn and become like little children, you will never enter the kingdom of heaven. Whoever humbles himself like this child, he is the greatest in the kingdom of heaven" (Mt. 8,3–4). This is clearly not about *remaining* a child, but about *becoming* a child. Even the disciples of Jesus, who love him and have committed themselves to him, who stand as his followers, have not yet grasped that. It has to be presented to them drastically. Certainly this child has nothing to show as accomplishment. He is still completely open to all discoveries. He lets himself be surprised from hour to hour and accepts help in everything that happens to him. Precisely what the child has by nature we must acquire in order to enter into the kingdom of heaven – apparently from the very nature of this kingdom. What in normal life is not achievement will be achievement there, even high achievement. In all the catalogs and systems of virtues which were put together by the great pre-Christian Greek masters we do not find any mention of becoming a child – neither as a specific virtue nor as a basic attitude. How surprising that is! For Jesus says it is the essential requirement for entrance into the kingdom of heaven.

A third statement of the Lord should be considered here. When the disciples came back from their first missionary journey, Jesus glorified the Father in these terms, "I thank you, Father, Lord of heaven and earth, that you have hidden these things from the wise and understanding and revealed them to babes; yes, Father, for such was your gracious will" (Lk. 10,21–22). Etymologically the "babes" means the children, the ones who cannot speak yet. And here more clearly than in the other two places the relationship to the Father is evident. If in the Old Testament God as Father and the poor are indeed present, but have not yet been linked, then here that linking is quite clear. The kingdom *is* the Father's kingdom. It is presented to human beings in a new birth. And the corresponding attitude is that of a child, full of trust and ready acceptance. The childlike attitude is conscious of its own littleness, incapacity, and helplessness; but it does not make a big deal about this, for that is not the important thing in its eyes. The important thing is the joyous acceptance that wells up from this frailty. It does not try to explain the frailty away or to ascribe to itself what is really a gift. Instead, it matter-of-factly carries out whatever commands or summonses may be entailed.

I do not know why the Fathers of Vatican II did not notice this connection between being poor and being a child in the teaching of Jesus. They racked their brains over what poverty as an evangelical attitude may mean today. They even came to conflict over it in reference to our welfare society and underdeveloped peoples. They said a lot that was thoughtful and sensible about this problem. But it never came into their heads to take the child as their starting point the way Jesus did in the midst of his disciples. And yet this wholly concrete approach says much more than any dry conceptual presentation of philosophy or theology.

Do I have to prove expressly that Francis of Assisi possessed the gospel childlikeness in a unique manner? It may be that no saint in the history of the Church is comparable to him in this respect. The *Dictionnaire de Spiritualité* says with lapidary conciseness: "In the thirteenth century the spirit of filial kinship was in some real way embodied in St. Francis and his first companions." For them it is "the way of perfection, which they found in the gospels." In the eyes of the Poverello, "Genuine and holy simplicity is the one noble and strong virtue.... Francis does not hesitate to associate it as a sister to Wisdom." Thus write François de Sainte-Marie and Charles Bernard, who appeal to Ivan Goby, the most important researcher on St. Francis in France today and also the author of the afore-mentioned monograph. But actually, you know, one does not need any such proof from authority. An unbiased look at his life is enough.

Of course we have to distinguish carefully between what one could call the childlike spirit of the Middle Ages (i. e., the real-life expression of a given cultural stage) and that which is signified by the basic Christian attitude of filial kinship that is found in the gospel. But distinguishing them from each other does not mean separating them. The one flows into the other. Every man exists in a definite cultural world, avails himself of its perceptions, its conceptual panoply, and its modes of expression, and he has only these at his disposal. Even when God wills to reveal himself, he is, so to speak, obliged to translate his truth into this cultural world. That causes the Scripture scholars of our day many difficulties and at times provokes us to laughter. For when we know them personally we see right away that they are people who can never feel their way into a milieu other than their own. For that reason their work of demythologizing is a poor patchwork from the start, despite all the immense learning they expend on it. In order to do the job really satisfactorily they would have to go through a fivefold process. (1) They would have to be able to completely detach themselves from their own milieu. (2) They would have to be able to get inside the life of a different milieu – that of early Christianity, for instance. (3) They would have to be able to experience God's revelation in this milieu. (4) They would have to be able to free the revelation from environmental factors. (5) They would have to be able to transpose it again to their present-day milieu. Only wholly simple people will be capable of going through these five steps completely – with a direct gaze that is intuitive rather than reflective. So in this case too, the Father reveals it to the little ones and the simple ones, but from the wise it remains hidden. In Thomas Aquinas I found the statement: "To be sure, the haughty perceive many hidden things with the intellect, but they do not get at the flavor. Even though they know how things are, they do not know how they taste." But the "taste" is exactly what must be arrived at in order to be able to transpose accurately.

I would like to cite an example of such intellectual misunderstanding here. In his book *Wandlungen der Seele im Hochmittelalter* (1936) Julius Schultz writes about Francis of Assisi:

"Childlikeness is the most original trait of this most appealing of all the saints. In his unholy youth he already attracted attention among his companions by eccentric clothes and manners; as assistant in his father's fabric business he delighted now and then in playfully sewing the most varied and unalike materials together into one garment. For days on end he lived in dreams of future greatness in which he naturally came off best. And as in those days he wanted to play the knight, so later he played with ardent compassion the witness of the passion of Christ.... Often he held intimate conversations with Christ, and so intensely did he imagine himself in his role of confidant, he believed he could hear the replies of God with his own ears. And then he went on to play this role before the whole world without shame – crying the message through the lanes, thanking God with a loud voice when boys smeared him with mud, and giving the impression of a madman. For the complete absence of shame in the face of the most compelling conventions, a sure sign of pathological infantilism, characterizes Francis as scarcely any other trait.... We can understand the enormous impact of this God-intoxicated beggar as flowing from precisely his childlike ingenuousness, in an age which could distinguish between holiness and mental disturbance much less sharply than our critical-minded present. But with this was paired childlike kindness: Francis disarmed church dignitaries and civil authorities, vicious enemies and even hostile bandits, by looking at them trustingly with his innocent eyes and proposing the unexpected as if it were the most natural thing in the world."

I believe many a contemporary person will think similarly if he reads the stories about Francis. He is captivated by the kindness of this man; he finds the playful element charming and unique, but at the same time he analyzes with a critical eye and finds "mental disturbance" and "pathological infantilism" to be characteristic tendencies.

Now I have no intention of saying in *a priori* fashion that pathological traits are not to be detected in the saints. In fact I would conjecture they are to be found in most of them. Saints are extraordinary people. Indeed we Christians say that the extraordinary element in them is a clear sign of the action of God. In a canonization process the Catholic Church places greatest importance on establishing the "heroic," i. e., extraordinary, degree of Christian virtues. Actually however, a certain eccentricity, a disturbance of the equilibrium that we call "normal" can indeed, and, in my opinion, will in fact, show up in the person's natural disposition. God's grace latches on to this in order to carry the person beyond himself. For all holiness elevates the human being beyond himself. Certainly this eccentricity can just as well degenerate into self-complacency, excessive pride, brutal egoism. But when it flows into service to fellowmen, into devotedness and self-forgetfulness, then it is precisely this extraordinariness, tamed and yet not rigid, harmonious and yet eccentric, that is the sign of the divine. Not that the extraordinary in itself amounts to that – rather the extraordinariness of the extraordinary does. That is to say, although there is dissonance, there is also harmony; although there is distortion, there is also balance; although there is ruin, there is also constructive effort. That is something a person can perhaps taste or savor. But he cannot calculate it, as I have already said.

After all, what is a "normal" person? Professor Rudin explores this question in his book *Psychotherapie und Religion* (1964). He points out how many-sided it is, depending on the standpoint from which we are approaching it: e. g., biology, medicine, psychology, anthropology, or philosophy. Then he goes on to point out quite rightly that we do not settle the question with a paltry abstraction "which regards human normality as an essence poured out countless times into the flask of a given phenotype." We must also take into account the "irreplaceable uniqueness and solitariness" of each individual. From the latter standpoint, all talk of the "normal" person seems to be "so much idle chatter, leading to nothing real or substantial."

Seen from this point of view, much in the childlikeness of Francis was nothing more than a phenomenon appropriate to the High Middle Ages. As a typical childlike person of the Middle Ages Francis was not distinct from others. His uniqueness is not to be found there. We should not consider this anthropological childlikeness as evangelical or as an ideal for the future. We have grown beyond it and that is good.

Surely something else is the case with the purely natural disposition of Francis. Here I must go back to the period before his conversion. Certainly it should be said at once that the "conversion," which he even speaks of himself in his *Testament,* was not at all the kind of experience which transformed a Saul into a Paul at Damascus. Rather, it was a psychic development which extended over a number of years.

On the whole, I tend to doubt that "conversions" ever occur in a flash. One always discovers that long before the so-called conversion-experience many lines of inner experience were tending in that direction. Even Paul tells us that he had kicked against the goad long before, and the Damascus experience by no means made him the later apostle; in between lay the contemplative period in the desert. Even an marvel of interior transformation does not fall like a meteor from heaven! A psychologist can speak of a long development which allows for a wholly natural explanation, however much others would like to see it as God's bolt from the blue.

In reality it is not that way. On the contrary, each person's life is a path which advances step by step in a continuing line, and the freedom of human decision does not lie at this or that place you can point to. Rather, freedom lies in a line with many intricacies that represents a constant question-and-answer game between God and man; in it God, like every lover, may appear under a thousand names. It is the line that makes the life. The decision lies in the line, in many respects hidden and perhaps never truly revealed until the end – like a bud from which the wrappings have not burst. In the "final decision," which people like to speak of today, that is, in the transition to the encounter with the unveiled, resurrected Christ, the bud may open. But where there is no bud, nothing can open. Where one does open, however, this final decision is literally the end result, the birth as it were of a being that was already there long before and slowly grew to maturity in the dark.

This is the way we have to look at Francis also. Some say he had been a frivolous young man, the uncrowned king within the circle of his companions because of his sparkling sallies and his drinking parties. A life-loving, gregarious young man without serious or loftier interests. But when we look more closely, we see this was not so. If I might use a present-day comparison, the young Francesco — so named because his much-traveled father Pietro Bernardone was enamored of Southern France and its troubadours — was very much a Beatle. The Beatles are eccentric characters, but not at all young people who simply enjoy life to the full. There are such youngsters too — pitiable, rootless young people, anti-social at the core. But the Beatles are not that. The Beatles represent a protest; their roots are a refusal to submit themselves to a society which they truly experience as a deception and an oppressive violation. Hence their success. For they put an emphatic finger on an actual wound in our society. They do this spontaneously and with a certain natural vitality. And a hundred thousand other people, who are not themselves equipped with the same energy to break out of the prison of the conventional or the constraints of a mechanized society, cheer them — because they too bear within themselves a secret prisoner whom they would be glad to give freedom if it were not for the terrible watchmen, "they" and "everybody," keeping guard at the door. Generals and other deserving men of society returned their titles of nobility and knighthood to Queen Elizabeth when she elevated the Beatles into their ranks. Nobody protested, however, when the same honor was bestowed upon Francis Chichester. And yet the "services" of Chichester and the Beatles are not so far apart when one considers their actions as two sides of the same coin or reflects upon their protests against contemporary society. Chichester's "great feat" of sailing around the world was a weird undertaking in our day. His protest is hopelessly out of date and oriented toward the past. The protest of the Beatles, on the other hand, is at bottom a protest against the enslaving of our own nature. Their protest is more amiable, but more dangerous, for it refers to the future.

The life of Francis of Assisi was such a protest. Even back then no man was more deceived and disappointed by him than his father. To be sure, father and son strove to emulate the position of knight and aristocrat, the position which held first place in society, in the fineness of their home and dress. In the last analysis it was a struggle for power. And yet, how different were the ways of father and son! Yes, even the goal. Money was the way for the father; how he acquired it wasn't very important. In other respects he remained within the frame of habits that were the external marks of the aristocratic man: good manners, a touch of courtly style, songs of chivalry, the French language. The son, by contrast, took all these things which had been bred into him and spontaneously looked for their inner meaning. He tried to savor their value as personal experiences.

Two examples. The young merchant's son was standing in the marketplace selling his father's fabrics. An elegant knight was interested, and in Italian style they began to haggle and bargain. During the lively exchange a poor man suddenly broke in requesting some trifle. Francis brushed him off impatiently; he was to wait. When the business with the knight was completed, Francis looked around for the poor man, but he had disappeared. Francis was unhappy. He asked the bystanders which way the man had gone. He left his stall – with all the merchandise laid out – and ran after him through the narrow and winding streets of the town. But he didn't find the man again. Francis was inconsolable. A human being was a human being, whether rich or poor. The one had as much right as the other. That is something his father would have never understood. Francis loved splendid clothes. But he might suddenly make a garment in which the costliest fabrics and miserable rags were blended chaotically, and, thus decked out, go walking around. A joke? Perhaps much more! Contempt for mere external show – a spontaneous judgment on the statement "clothes make the man," and an inner need to make this "principle" plainly ridiculous.

Somewhat later, after his long illness, he wanted to take part in a military campaign in Southern Italy. He wanted to distinguish himself in it, and that would bring him knighthood according to the custom of the time. Night and day he dreams boyishly of this expedition. He has a magnificent suit of armor made for himself. Then a few days before his departure, he comes upon an impoverished nobleman who also wants to go but cannot afford the equipment. Francis – without any ado – gave him his own armor. We have here the same phenomenon. Being a knight is an inner attitude; the equipment is only an external expression which can fall by the wayside. Francis' proverbial extravagance is also, it seems to me, not so much carelessness as a disdain for money – as if he wanted to say: "That doesn't matter at all; the true worth of a person lies elsewhere."

We still have much more to say about money in the life of the saint, but here it is enough to indicate that he never was addicted to money. The style of his disregard simply changed.

So there we have the Beatle Francis. I have yet to see an old Beatle. Being a Beatle is something typical of the young; it bespeaks an immediacy and spontaneity that provokes solid and settled people. Yes, in it lies the shocking honesty of a child. As Heinrich Spaemann said: "The child is a merry, irreverent assault of reality on unreality, so it exposes the nonsense and impotence of unreality." Grownups speak apologetically of the *enfant terrible* – yet cannot help but love him.

Something of this childlikeness always remained in Francis. Even the "conversion" did not rob him of that. I find it injudicious and silly to speak here of pathological infantilism. To a psychologist it may seem at first glance to be that. But the Christian will not be able to speak that way. Only total openness to God, which leaves aside all "ifs" and "buts," which does not let itself be hampered by any kind of prejudice about "what people do," opens the gate of the kingdom of heaven. In the perception of this truth Francis remained no child. Precisely in that lay his conversion. It is amazing how each of the encounters in which he believed he clearly understood the voice of the Lord was preceded by a period of intensive reflection. In one case it was his long illness; in another, the many visits to the hidden cave in which, as he told a friend, "a treasure lay concealed"; and in another, the life in hiding from his persecuting father. Later, and no less importantly, came the long periods of solitary living that are such an essential part of the figure of Francis. Make no mistake about it – in these long periods of prayer Francis became a man. They were an extremely hard struggle, and he came from his prayer periods completely changed. He was terrible to see. Nevertheless, as paradoxical as it may sound, in this inner struggle Francis first *became* a child in the gospel sense, the child the gospel instructs us to be.

Before Francis became a despiser of money – an almsgiver – he had a heart for the poor; he also had a feel for the inner meaning of authentic knighthood. Later he was a poor man himself, and Poverty was his beloved bride. When the Bishop of Assisi suggested to him that his radical poverty was too difficult, Francis replied: "My Lord, if we wish to possess something, then we have to have weapons for our defense. From that comes the quarrels and struggles which in so many ways hinder love of God and fellowmen. Therefore we choose to possess nothing temporal in the world." This answer cut the Bishop to the quick, for he was an extremely contentious man when worldly goods were involved.

Years later, when Francis was soon to die and lay seriously ill in the convent garden of the sisters of St. Clare, the same Bishop, who always admired Francis immensely, was embroiled in a violent argument with the Mayor of Assisi. Francis summoned the two – the Bishop and the Mayor – and also the whole town to the plaza in front of the Bishop's palace. He sent two friars there. They sang the so-called "Canticle of the Sun," to which Francis had attached a new verse: "All praise be yours, my Lord, through those who grant pardon for love of you; through those who endure sickness and trial. Happy those who endure in peace; by you, Most High, they will be crowned." And what was the effect? The Bishop had excommunicated the Mayor; the Mayor

Picture page 37:
Valley of Rieti with the poplars that are typical of that area. On his first missionary journey Francis went through this region and preached repentance. Writes Jörgensen: "Even today in Rieti one is justified in seeing Francis' preaching there as a work of evangelization in the authentic meaning of the word — i. e., as a conversion from paganism to Christianity."

Picture pages 38–39:
On one occasion Francis came to a village church in the environs of Assisi (on the east slope of Subasio). There he began to sweep out the church. The news spread quickly. A simple farmer named Giovanni was plowing a field, not far from the church, and noticed him. He came at once and said: "Give me the broom. I want to help you." After they had finished the job, they sat down together. Giovanni said: "It was God's will that I run into you. I should like to do what you think is best." Francis replied: "If you choose to share our life, then you must give away all you possess to the poor."
Giovanni went over to the oxen he had left standing nearby and brought one of them to Francis: "Give him to the poor. He is portion of the family inheritance." Francis laughed. Giovanni's parents and younger brothers and sisters came running and pleaded to have the ox back. Francis said to them: "I'll give you back the ox and take your brother." And that is what he did.

Bas-relief from the lower church of San Pietro in Spoleto (5th cent.).

Picture page 40:
Landscape facing Ancona in The Marches (Le Marche). Francis had gathered three companions around him. In the summer of 1209 they decided to split up. Francis took Egidio with him, heading towards the Ancona region of The Marches. The other two went off in a different direction. As they walked along, they exulted in the Lord and Francis sang "bright, clear songs in praise of the Almighty." They were songs in the local dialect. The travellers were convinced that they had found "the treasure in the field" of which the Gospel speaks.

had forbidden the selling of anything to the Bishop, buying from him, or entering into a contract with him. It was a public scandal. But at this simple song the Mayor wept and pardoned the Bishop. The Bishop said: "In my office it is fitting that I be humble. But because by nature I am inclined to argue, you should have kind indulgence toward me." And the two embraced each other.

This Bishop appears as a counterpoint to Francis. On the basis of the documents, Arnaldo Fortini is of the opinion that he "clearly had an unbridled attachment to earthly things, confused the sacred and the secular, approved prayers and offerings for vineyards and mules, and assured himself of paradise through transfer of a piece of land." His opinion of anyone who opposed him was, "Let him be cursed like Nathan and Abiron, who were swallowed up by the earth." This Bishop, who was a good pastor, is not an isolated case. We still have his kind today, and not infrequently. It is necessary to see him as background in order to understand what it meant for Francis to become a child – why he saw poverty as freedom and why to him this seemed to be grounded in the gospel.

Perhaps you will ask what all this has to do with our time. Obviously we are not being commanded to return to the childlike Middle Ages. We may be amazed by and love the poetry of this childlikeness. We may regret that this enchanting bloom of medieval simplicity has vanished. But this fragrant rose no longer thrives in our atmosphere. It is senseless to try to grow it artificially today.

That could make us somewhat modest, we who frequently imagine we are in all respects head and shoulders above earlier periods. We have made progress – to deny that or give it up would be foolish. But at the same time we must not forget that any progress demands a price. Opposite a gain stands a loss. No one should deny that either. During Vatican II there arose in world opinion stereotyped conceptions of the progress of the world, of the Church, and of the Church in the contemporary world, which could come close to arrogance even when they were concerned with "service." In short they evoked the impression that everything up to now has been darkness and confusion. It is understandable that this impression developed. Anyone who wants to achieve something depicts the inadequacy of what has gone before. Inferiority complexes have always been motors for progress.

Nevertheless, after the breakthrough to new consciousness, we must adopt a critical spirit toward it. In the name of the critical spirit we choose to break through the boundaries of the old. Custom and tradition have built a multitude of such boundaries around us. We have acquired genuine, new findings through modern sciences, but for a long time we did not dare go against certain taboos of the past. But today young people especially are breaking through these taboos and wiping them out – taboos in our outlook on authority, morality, social order, the relationship between the sexes, and so on. The establishment offers resistance, but the new sciences go along – often reluctantly. Even before the circumstances change, people's awareness has changed. First off, every restriction is challenged. It does not count anymore that "things have always been so." If "that's what people have always said," then it is surely open to suspicion. That the Church says so does not matter much even to the faithful. Critical awareness is everything.

But what is critical awareness? Is it a completely unprejudiced view of things? Isn't it often these days a prejudiced judgment? Is it the matter-of-fact attitude of the impartial and therefore solely critical child? Or again, is it blind yea-saying to everything that a science has proposed as "hypothesis" or "model"?

We no longer have, and will not have again, the childlike spirit of the Middle Ages which unquestioningly accepted everything it was told. But for that reason we must hang on still longer to the ingenuousness of the incorruptible child, whose mind cannot be manipulated, and to whom the chasing of every trend is alien. Many people consider themselves to be completely unprejudiced when they try group sex, for example. But if they notice then that something strong and permanent in them offers resistance, they take refuge in reflections that are conditioned by preconceived ideas. They say that what's operative here is the false education of the milieu in which they were raised. But how do they know that? It may just as well be eros operating: the attraction between the sexes which hinders self-becoming in group sex, whereas in the sole possession of a partner it finds fulfillment. As I see it, self-critical childlikeness was not meant to be bound up with a given time or rooted in a single era. Maybe it will always be a rare flower, but it will always be a flower.

Now the astonishing thing is that this *critical* childlike sense was part and parcel of Francis of Assisi. That's where we get his hippie-style rebellion which we were talking about before, and his unconcern about all barriers, even ecclesiastical barriers, in the formation of his new community. It was the critical eye that led him – surely not the eye of science, but the eye of a child. He never lost it. It shone most beautifully where one least expects it: in his relationship with Clare, who loved to call herself her brother's plant. Their relationship was completely unacceptable for that age, and yet it was thoroughly understood precisely by simple people. It was true eros, sublimated in the spiritual, free of any animalistic drive, but not freed from being a genuine man-woman encounter. Francis was honored – yes, loved – by Clare, the distinguished daughter of an aristocratic family. He returned the love.

The love was not platonic. Clare was no "idea" for him – of the eternally feminine, for instance. Nor was she a figure of the virgin Mother of God, as we find with other saints in their relationships with women. Neither was she that sorrowful re-enactment of the Cross which Paul Claudel movingly tried to depict time and again: painful renunciation of all ties to the beloved, who is then found again in a higher, spiritual, but always still personal sense. Such a refined but extremely intellectual approach would scarcely have been possible.

He had taken upon himself the evangelical counsel about remaining unmarried for the sake of the kingdom. At times one would like to believe him caught up in his mystical world to such a degree that he was never touched by bodily sexual impulses. But then one reads the strange tale of the seven snowmen, which in a moment of sexual temptation he built in the garden.

"There is the wife, there are the four children, there is the manservant, and there is the woman-servant – and what has become of the undivided devotion to God?" Thus he overcame the protest of the flesh. And oftentimes, when people extolled him as a saint, he is supposed to have said, "How do you know that I will not have children yet?" So in that respect he was a man of flesh and blood, and no different from the other saints of history. His renunciation of marriage was a part of his poverty, as tangible and real as his renunciation of material fortune.

But Clare was another matter. She did not stand in the way of his undivided devotion to his task. On the contrary, Clare complemented, sheltered, and strengthened him in it. But don't think he saw in Clare only a "human being" he had won for the gospel, a person who happened incidentally to be a woman. Anything but! He loved the woman in her and he loved her as a woman. The difference is perceptible if you compare his love for the friars and his relation to Clare's two sisters to his relationship with her. Even the other woman who played an important role in his life (and especially at the moment of his death), Jacoba di Settesoli, has a completely different relationship to him than Clare. The sensitive, solicitous, motherly admirer he calls "Brother Jacoba" is like a brother to him, comparable to the other brothers – and for that reason she is even permitted to enter their cloister. Clare he never called "Brother Clare." With Clare's sisters he is just as reserved as with women generally, even though they left their parent's home to join Clare's community under dramatic circumstances which took far wilder form than Clare's flight.

But in the case of Clare one gets the impression that only consideration of people's gossip caused him to become a rare guest after the first period of frequent visits. Only the incorruptible eye of the child could assure him that a unique relationship existed here which did not stand in the way of celibacy. Now Clare was without doubt an outstanding woman. In Francis and from him she came to know the ideal of her life. But Jörgensen may well be correct when he writes: "No one embodies more perfectly the ideal of a man than a woman who is moved by that same ideal.... If one wants to see the Franciscan life in a figure free of all alien influences and the later requirements added perforce, then he must turn to Francis' great womanly pupil, the saintly Clare of Assisi. She even loved to call herself her brother's plant. She is indeed the flower of the Franciscan Order."

It is a fact that Francis again and again felt drawn to Clare in all the difficult and critical moments of his life. When he is in doubt whether he should give up his preaching activity in favor of a purely contemplative life, he puts the question to Clare. She decides: you are there for others. Before he undergoes the fearful eye operation, he cannot refrain from taking leave of Clare. For fifteen days he lies in a bamboo hut in the garden of San Damiano, the convent in which Clare is superior. More firmly and unequivocally than Francis, Clare opposes church authorities on the poverty question. "I will not be dispensed from the gospel," was her reply when they wanted to make the rule milder. On the other hand, Clare trembles with fear and anxiety when she herself is very ill and afraid she may die before Francis. The thought is unbearable to her.

There is a folk legend which depicts this relationship better than all the theories. It goes as follows. Francis with Friar Leo had been badly received in Siena. It was evening when they, dead-tired, left the city heading in the direction of Assisi. Francis was thinking of "his" town and of Clare, the daughter of his heart. The darker it became the more anxious he felt about Clare. He knew that Cardinal Ugolino wanted to force his own rule, similar to that of the Benedictine nuns, upon Clare's sisters. Will Clare remain strong? She stood alone. Francis had the feeling his feet would sink into the earth at every moment. They came to a spring of drinking water. The water was clear; from the pipe a stream fell on the surface of the water in the trough. For a long time Francis stood motionless, bent over the water. Then suddenly he lifted his head happily and said to his companion, "Brother Leo, little lamb of God, what do you think I have seen in the water?"

"I suppose the moon," answered the friar. "It is reflected in the water."

"No, Brother Leo, I did not see our Sister Moon in the water. Through the grace of the Lord I saw the real-life countenance of our Sister Clare. It was so pure, and radiated such holy joy, that all my doubts flew away at once. Now I am quite certain that at this moment she is filled with the deep joy God gives his friends."

A union like that – existing beyond separation in space – attests to that clear eye of which the gospel says, "If your eye is sound, your whole body will be full of light." It is what is meant by the Johannine acclamation of Christ in Matthew: "I thank you, Father, that you have hidden these things from the wise and understanding and revealed them to babes." And it is precisely that "discernment of spirits" which is given only to children, which will always remain hidden from the pansexualists of our day.

3. Living the Gospel

Today we are rather proud of *Dei Verbum,* the Constitution on Divine Revelation of Vatican II. It may well have left open the initial quarrel over the relationship of Sacred Scripture and tradition which split the Council into two hostile camps and threatened to plunge Non-Catholic observers into deep disappointment. It may well have left unanswered many desirable and in fact urgent requests of current scholarly exegesis. Nevertheless it is looked upon, even by many Protestants, as one of the most beautiful council documents, and as one of the most promising for the future. It breathes a spirit which transcends the petty disputes that of course seem extremely important to scholars but spoil the flavor for believing Christians. And for this very reason one gets the feeling that this spirit can indeed create life. I say "create" – not "calculate laboriously through infinitely tangled paths."

How does the Council manage to convey this feeling? It does so by approximating as simply as possible the mode of expression and sayings of Holy Scripture in its statements, and by speaking about Scripture with genuine and clearly high esteem. Anyone can see that Holy Scripture is a highest value and supreme norm to the men who wrote this text. The only similar text is in the first chapter of the Constitution on the Liturgy, but that too deals with Holy Scripture in large measure. There was another similar text in one draft of the so-called "Schema on the Jews," but the fresh vigor of Scripture bearing witness to itself was lost in the further work of editing even though all the essential statements were in the final version. The Dogmatic Constitution on Divine Revelation, however, managed to achieve this vigor over the course of several years deliberation. Some people have attributed this to the Catholic Biblical movement which got its start under Pius XII. Undoubtedly this is one of the sources, if not *the* source of the ecumenical movement within the Catholic Church.

The cry "back to the sources" was to begin with a cry of the scholarly sciences. It came after all the efforts under Leo XIII to give new life to scholasticism proved on the whole, despite success in the beginning, an impractical way to start a dialogue with the modern world. Strangely enough, the movement didn't return directly to Holy Scripture, but first of all to the patristic period. It was not unjustly said that at that time in its transmission the stream of revelation had not yet been channelled into the narrow bed of later periods. This "patristic renaissance" reached its high point in the so-called *théologie nouvelle.* In his encyclical *Humani generis* Pius XII certainly did not intend to stifle this new theology, rather to channel it correctly. But in fact he put the brakes on it. Now for the first time the Biblical movement appeared more strongly in the foreground. It had a broader as well as a deeper motivation than the patristic revival. It was broader because it did not just involve the narrow sphere of educated people or specialists; it also involved countless groups of Bible readers scattered throughout the whole people of God. It was deeper because the Bible was not only a reflection of the word of God, but this word itself. The science of Bibilical scholarship followed only gradually in the Catholic Church – because it was handicapped by many decrees of Roman authorities. But in an age of scholarly science it was inevitable that a movement which little by little excited the whole body of the Church gradually overcame this obstacle as well. Hesitantly but unmistakably Pius XII made an opening with a pertinent encyclical. Bit by bit the structure of the Roman Biblical commission changed. The whole atmosphere grew more free.

That could not get off the ground without coming to grips with tradition; for in the last analysis the Church regarded herself as the living transmission of divine revelation, an authentic transmission vouchsafed to her by her founder. This transmission included not only the preservation of a book but also its explanation and interpretation, and indeed is fruitful embodiment and concrete realization. This assistance of the founder extended to the Church as a whole, to all those united in her. Authority in the Church had to be an expression of her consciousness as a whole; it could never be opposed to this. Authority did not create tradition. In itself it was not tradition; it was only a function of service within tradition.

Viewed in this light, Holy Scripture itself turned out to be a unique and singular element of tradition. The authority of the Church did not compose Holy Scripture. Representatives of authority may or may not be among the authors of the holy books. What gives the books their special and unique value is not church authority, but the special help and quality stamped upon them by Christ's promise, "I will be with you all days," which he in sovereign freedom granted to individuals in this Church. This is also true of the authors and authorities of the Old Covenant, for even during these ages the promised Messiah was already operative within his people.

Now it has ever been the case that the uniqueness of Holy Scripture resides in the fact that it is God's saving deed in history, for all Christians and all times, comparable to nothing else. Not only is it the guidepost around which all Christian life is to grow; it is also the direct source of life-giving forces. Thus Holy Scripture cannot be placed over against the Church, and certainly not over against authority in the Church. This has always been true, as we just remarked, but now people began to experience the uniqueness of Holy Scripture more clearly. They became aware that this testimonial record of the deeds and words of God belonged to the living arteries and cell structure of the people of God. It was not only the yardstick to be applied anywhere in order to measure the authenticity of all Christian life and activity; it was also that through which and out of which new life continually came forth. Within the Church Holy Scripture is the manifestation of the assistance Christ promised eternally to her, just as – and in fact even more so than – the visible sacramental signs and structures attached perpetually to the Church are. To play them off against one another, or even simply to separate them clearly in the conceptual realm, is scarcely a feasible undertaking. They are entwined with one another. They are a living totality from which the life escapes as soon as you try to examine one "part" separately.

I do not wish to suggest that the Church has not been constantly aware of this. Nevertheless there were shifts of emphasis in the course of history. At times – especially in the consciousness of simple believers – they bordered on a perversion of the true order. A person "nourished" the faith on catechisms and church definitions, on sermons and pious literature of a popular sort. Of course there remained the texts of the Sunday liturgy, but they were only a small segment. The entirety of the accumulated, historical revelation of God was scarcely given its due consideration. So Holy Scripture turned into a mysterious book, a veiled picture, which it was not desirable to examine directly and which seemed rather dangerous. This period, caused perhaps by the defensive position of the Catholic Church vis-a-vis the Reformation, is past today – so much so that now a new obstacle of a completely different sort confronts the Bible reader.

Scholarly science has taken possession of the Bible. For in the Bible "God's words" – formulated by human tongues – have become analogous to human utterances, as once the Word of the eternal Father became like man by taking on frail human flesh. So it is extremely difficult to discover what a passage of the New Testament or the Old Testament really intends to say now – i. e., in our terms. A new veil lies over Holy Scripture; and looking at it directly appears to be a very dangerous procedure unless one approaches it in the protective accouterments of modern historical and linguistic scholarship. It seems no easier to read the Bible than to visit the moon.

In the conciliar constitution *Dei Verbum* the Church does of course say that Holy Scripture is "the supreme rule" of its faith; and without reservation she demands that "easy access to Sacred Scripture should be provided for all the Christian faithful." Study of the holy books should be "the soul of sacred theology." All the Christian faithful should "learn by frequent reading of the divine Scriptures the 'excelling knowledge of Jesus Christ' (Phil. 3,8). For ignorance of the Scripture is ignorance of Christ'" (n. 25).

All that is right and good – but this "dialogue with the Father in heaven" seems to be extremely difficult indeed if I have to read a book of interpretation, full of incomprehensible words, in order to understand every line of this "letter from God" to me. Doesn't that seal up anew the pure source? And because the science here referred to is full of hypotheses, conjectures, and doubts like every other science, won't our faith seem like an unstable and bookish faith without much strength and life in it?

I am not pulling the difficulty raised here out of the air. It is a very concrete difficulty weighing heavily on many Christians, who only slowly and hesitantly pick up Holy Scripture. The objection should not be shoved aside too quickly as irrelevant and immaterial. It is of course only a practical objection. But the fact is that the important thing for Christians to do is to achieve a real effective dialogue with the God who speaks to them in Scripture. And there a practical difficulty can outweigh many theoretical "problems."

And in fact, did not the same Second Vatican Council in our own day speak of the necessity in the Church of the many charisms which God freely bestows? In the speeches of the bishops one heard the oft-repeated lament that such charisms were for all practical purposes dead among the laity. Many said that the charisms of the laity had not been able to develop properly because of the exaggeration of the principle of authority in the last one hundred and fifty years. That may well be. But perhaps the answer must be spelled out still further. Perhaps we must say that we have not put Scripture into the hands of the laity enough. The special gifts of grace and initiative of laity and religious alike develop precisely through the meditation of believers, through reflection on Sacred Scripture in their hearts, in which God conducts a "dialogue" with them – just as Scripture itself grew out of such reflection. That is to say, it is not a textbook, but a living witness. But then the question is, how is that to continue happening today?

Here I see the Poverello of Assisi as a peerless example. For his relationship to the gospel is of an immediacy and intimacy unmatched by any other religious community. At first glance this statement may seem to be an exaggeration, and I will admit that I took it for that when I came across it in books and articles by representatives of the Franciscan family. Every order is obligated to follow Christ in accordance with the gospel in the long run, I said to myself. Every founder of an order has tried to translate the gospel to his time and particular circumstances. Many have then oriented their organizations to a definite purpose such as nursing the sick, opening schools, ransoming slaves, but always in the spirit of the gospel. Others have not chosen any special goal for their orders, but simply have tried to flesh out the gospel by following the evangelical counsels in accordance with their situation. However all of them – even the modern secular institutes, which are not religious orders and consciously do not want to be – live according to the so-called "evangelical counsels." That is the core common to all. For that reason the Council's *Decree on the Appropriate Renewal of Religious Life* said: "Since the fundamental norm of the religious life is the following of Christ as proposed by the gospel, such is to be regarded by all communities as their supreme law."

That is all very true and correct. Yet Francis of Assisi shows an "evangelical" note, an immediacy to the gospel, which has also carried over to his order in a way not characteristic of the others. Perhaps we can simply say: *Francis wanted nothing else but to live the gospel.* We are accustomed to seeing in him "the *Poverello*," the man of poverty. In fact he did once make a statement about poverty similar to Ignatius of Loyola's later statement about obedience. Nevertheless it would be just as false to see in Francis a poverty fanatic, or even a theoretician of poverty, as to imagine obedience to be the core of Ignatius' spirituality. Certainly Ignatius said in his letter on obedience he would rather the Jesuits excel other orders in obedience than in any virtue. That was very serious to him. All the same this obedience was for him, strictly speaking, only the indispensable safeguard of a highly personal and individual imitation of Christ based on the discernment of spirits. Likewise Francis said, "The example of the poverty of God's son must obligate us more than all other orders." Here again, it is not poverty as such that is his concern; he obviously speaks of it only because he believes he has found it in the gospel. What he actually wants is the gospel and nothing but the gospel.

This can be proved in many ways. Let me sketch the bare outlines.

The hour of conversion actually first struck for Francis in that experience at Spoleto, whither he had marched with others in order to earn for himself, a merchant's son, recognition as a knight in the service of a secular master. "Who can reward you better, the master or the servant?" he thought he heard the Lord ask. "Why do you attach yourself to a man who is only a 'servant' himself, instead of going to him who is the Lord?" This was obviously the breakthrough of an inner light which he had vainly sought during his long illness after the unsuccessful expedition against Perugia, the hereditary enemy of Assisi. Up to now, because of his environment and upbringing, his thinking had been traveling on an entirely different path. It was, so to speak, his "tower experience," a piece of knowledge which was not at all theoretical but wholly existential. Or should we say his "Damascus experience"? We do not know whether at that time Francis was acquainted with the conversion of Saul. Still the parallel is close. The twenty-five year old Francis also asks, "Lord, what would you have me do?" And he receives in answer: "Go back to Assisi. I will fulfill your vision (a dream which had carried him on a knightly quest) in a spiritual way."

That happened in the year 1205. What follows next are partly picturesque, partly dramatic episodes. They contributed greatly to the development of the young man. They brought a serious note to his hitherto playful existence, and replaced the romantic dream with hard reality. Amid all this turbulence it is easy to forget what fundamentally is going on in Francis during this period: he is waiting to learn what he should do, and he does not find the answer. That was a very painful time.

If I am not mistaken, here the biographers have confused the whole matter through all kinds of anachronisms. They relate that once back from Spoleto – amid all the excitement and fanfare especially dear to young people in a small town – Francis was different than before. He acted like a man in love. His heart was no longer in the affair. The others noticed it, teased him about it, and he conceded openly: "Yes, you are right! I am in love." And he proudly added, "My intended bride is richer, more noble, and more lovely than anyone you have ever set eyes on." Right off the bat the biographers know that this intended bride is "Lady Poverty." That is what Francis had in mind. His whole inner development is behind him. But if this had already been settled for the young man, nothing could have kept him from immediately giving away all his fortune. However he did not do that. Then who was the bride? It was precisely the realization of his vision, or the true service of God, which was promised him and which he still awaited! He was in love with his betrothed, whom he did not yet know but who definitely was promised to him by the one who is the real Lord.

His experience with the leper is no different. It does give him an inner experience for his whole life, but it does not give an answer. He speaks of a "treasure in a cave," and he spends long hours there every day. Only one friend knows about it. But what takes place in the cave? Francis prays and sings in the company of God. The "treasure" is neither poverty nor any other "virtue." It is whatever the true Master wishes Francis to do. It must be something great; that is clear to him. But what? Often he comes out of the cave totally bewildered. He does not find the answer.

In this discouraging state of affairs he considers a pilgrimage to Rome; and because he is a man whose soul and body are so naturally one, he in fact goes there. Maybe the "answer" will dawn on him at the tombs of the apostles. He took plenty of money along with him. When he saw that the other upper-class pilgrims laid such paltry, well-calculated gifts on the altar of Peter, he threw down handfuls of money; for a fit of anger had seized him at the stinginess of the rich people. He was ashamed to be one of them. He tore off his rich clothes and sat as a beggar among the beggars for a day. He was one of them. Were they not better people? On the other hand, a pious old crone in the church at Assisi was fearfully disgusting to him. That was not what he wanted to be now or ever. So his thoughts changed little by little. What until now had been bitter became sweet to him, the sweet bitter. Undoubtedly he had made steps forward in his inner life. But all that was not the promised spiritual fulfillment of the light which had broken in at Spoleto.

It may be that Guido, the Bishop of Assisi, advised him to take this pilgrimage, for the biographers all report that he was visiting the Bishop frequently during that period to get advice from him. The Bishop, who as I already mentioned displayed an often extraordinary and downright avaricious attitude in worldly affairs (naturally in the interest of the Church) and was a man very prone to anger, dealt with Francis very wisely. He was a first-class spiritual director. Apparently his counsel was quite insightful, for they say Francis often came from him comforted. On the other hand, Guido did not anticipate the action of God. He certainly hoped Francis would decide to become a priest or a member of an order. However he never spoke of that and allowed his protégé complete freedom. He marveled greatly at the young man, and his sympathy was completely on his side. Later, in the affair with Clare and other matters, this will prove of great advantage to Francis (for example, in the aforementioned quarrel with the mayor). That was a bishop who in spite of many gross failings still had the greatest respect for charisms in the Church, even when that brought him into conflict with the aristocrats of the diocese or with public opinion. The solution, however, was not forthcoming from the Bishop either.

This is most clearly evident in that series of events which begins with the prayers before the crucifix in the little church of San Damiano and ends in the highly dramatic scene in which Francis lays his clothes at the feet of the Bishop. The general view is that the decisive change in the life of Francis of Assisi occurred here. However that is not the case. It is true though that a new stage in the search for the "mistress," the "bridge," or the "spiritual way" in which Francis intends to serve God, begins now – the search for his authentic mandate and mission.

What did happen? The half-desperate Francis believes he hears these words directed to him from the Cross: "Go and rebuild my church. You see it is all in ruins." One may wonder whether the high-spirited young man might not have thought of the Catholic Church of his day when he heard this "my church." This thought strikes us more quickly than the thought of the dilapidated little church of San Damiano, to all appearances hardly a critical center of pastoral activity. But for Francis it was otherwise. All abstract thinking was alien to him. He lived through everything in a concrete and wholly personal way. In his book on Francis, which seems to me to be the most well-thought-out introduction to the spirituality of the saint, the Franciscan Erich Rohr points out that St. Francis' thinking did not readily proceed from abstract concepts. We shall have to come back to this character trait later. Here it is brought up simply so we may realize that, for Francis, "my church" was first and foremost the concrete, existing little church of San Damiano.

Maybe he regarded this as his "test" in the service of God – just as knighthood required a test of fidelity and service. So he did not ask for long whether it was meaningful and purposeful, an important matter or not. He was glad to have a concrete duty for himself, and with his characteristic generosity he set to work. He instructed the priest on duty in the church to burn a perpetual light before the Cross. He sold a large bale of his father's cloth in Foligno and also the horse he had ridden there. He offered the money to the priest for the restoration of the little church. The man was highly disconcerted and alarmed. Today many people suppose he was a Waldensian. Perhaps he had been transferred to the wretched job for more or less disciplinary reasons. The money could make a lot of trouble for him. He didn't want to hear anything about it. But Francis placed it abruptly on the window sill of the chapel. He also asked the priest for permission to live with him from then on. The priest agreed. And so it begins, Francis thought. What? He still really did not know that himself. That was still to come. The only thing now is to pass the "test"!

As everyone knows, his father returned home soon after that and was, understandably enough, furious at the foolish deeds of his son. Francis, by no means a hero as his uncertainty shows, hid himself in the forest. There someone brought him a bit of food.

Weeks later he finally managed to pluck up courage. Deathly pale and emaciated, he ventured out. But interiorly he was happy, for that surely was to be the test of his fidelity. He was like a madman to look upon as he went through the little town. The children jeered and threw mud at him. He bore that without showing even the least agitation. His father rushed out of the house, hauled in his son, and thrashed him soundly. What father would not have done the same? Then he locked him in. Since he had to leave again on a business trip, he also chained him hand and foot. The madman had to be brought to his senses. That sounds fairly barbarous – but they did not know about depth psychology in those days, and shock therapy is basically not much more humane. However, his mother Pica was there and she let her son loose again because she believed in him.

The second encounter, when Pietro Bernardone returned, was substantially more moderate. No doubt the mother's tempering had an effect. The father rushed to the little church where his son sat peacefully before the door. A sharp exchange of words followed. "For all I care you can run after your crazy idea," cries the father beside himself, "but the money has to be returned, and I want nothing more to do with the whole story." But Francis had no intention of giving back the money. It no longer belonged to him; it was the property of the Church. Thus the whole story came before the Bishop – inasmuch as Francis no longer recognized a secular court. He was now in the service of the Church, and we already know that the Bishop was a friend and confidant of the young Bernardone.

It came to legal proceedings in the public plaza. The Bishop directed the young man to give the money back, and remarked bitingly: "God does not want his Church to be helped with money that was perhaps unjustly acquired." The cutting remark of the angry prelate hit home. He admonished Francis to trust in God who would repay him for service to his Church. Francis now anticipated his father's threat of disinheritance. He took off his clothing and laid it with the money at the feet of the Bishop. Then he said: "My Lord, I want to return not only the money that belongs to him but also the clothes which are his." He then turned to the people and cried: "Listen all of you, and understand what I say. Until today I have called Pietro Bernardone my father. But since I intend to serve the Lord, I return to him the money which causes him so much worry and agitation, and also all the clothing which I had from him. From now on I will say 'Our Father in heaven', not 'My father Pietro Bernardone.'"

That was a scene! Worthy in staging and manner of any knightly tale. It has not been neglected by painters. They have portrayed it again and again – Giotto best of all. However with this event, which the young man slid into more than sought, his problem was not solved. What about the promising commission to rebuild "my church"? He was being disinherited from his father; he certainly had no money at his disposal. He had no choice but to do the work by his own hands. How – that he didn't know. He still had no hint of a clear mandate.

That is evident, above all, in the considerable amount of aimless wandering that he now did. He goes as far as Gubbio to visit a friend who clothes him in pilgrim style: tunic, leather belt, sandals, and a staff. When robbers beat him up on the way to Gubbio, stripped him of his clothes, and tossed him into a snow pit, he indeed had said: "I am the herald of a great king." But what that meant he did not know. Now he turned back toward San Damiano. The priest there took him in and gave him plenty to eat. Francis labored, begged stones – worked on rebuilding the church. The longer it went on, the stronger his doubt grew: this surely could not be what was expected of him! He stopped accepting food from the priest. Instead he begged that also, so that everything would not seem so carefree and easy. After the first church, he restored a second; after the second, a third. The situation became more and more problematical.

I can well understand why a priest leading a pilgrimage of Third Order members said to them: "Francis himself didn't know what he wanted, and his followers still don't know today." The good man knew for certain only the facts I have just narrated, which are indeed quite confusing. He had not taken the trouble to distinguish the line of Francis' spiritual development. Perhaps he had read one or another of the many little brochures like those offered for sale in Assisi. They attempt to explain for the pilgrim the individual places he can visit there: for instance, the grave with the magnificent paintings by Giotto and Cimabue, the birthplace, the old cathedral, San Damiano, Portiuncula. But what contradictory associations are interwoven in all that! I have never had to make such an effort to feel my way into the spiritual development of a saint as with St. Francis. A bit of poetic earthiness, a touch of amazing kindness, a few beautiful emotions compounded of sympathy and admiration, a poetic garland of legends which exactly suit the enchanting Umbrian landscape: all these are part of the picture, but one's work does not end there. And yet when I told a scholarly Dominican, whom I respect a great deal, that I intended to write a book about St. Francis, I was surprised at his spontaneous reply: "St. Francis? Well, there's complete confusion!" And indeed it does seem that way.

Maybe the reader will now understand why I seem to have strayed so far from the theme in this chapter. It was in order to indicate the course Francis followed in his development. I wanted to let the reader participate in that; for only someone who has gone along the tangled path, anxious over the outcome, can come close to understanding the end of the story. The ending is indeed quite simple and perhaps even primitive, but it did in fact resolve the mysterious promise of Spoleto. It marks Francis' later way of life much more than all that has gone before; it determines the particular character of his community. However much it may have been blurred or overlaid with foreign elements, right down to today it continues to influence everything that we are wont to call "Franciscan," be it their theology, their pastoral work, their outlook on life, or their spirituality. What I say is nothing new. People like Hilarin Felder have seen it and said it long since – but perhaps they did not fully succeed in formulating their insight in such a way that it would strike home. For they made an abstraction out of it – and that just does not suit Francis of Assisi.

So let us get to the ending. It happened on February 24, 1209 (1208), almost four (five) years exactly since the dream at

Spoleto. (The dream was before mid-1205 because the Norman Walter de Brienne, the leader of the troops in Apulia who were loyal to the Pope and whom Francis wanted to join, died in June of that year.) Francis' restoration of the church of Portiuncula was as good as finished. The feast of St. Matthew the Apostle was to be celebrated there. On such days a priest came to say Mass. Francis was in attendance. According to the missal of that time, the Gospel for the day was Matthew 10,7–20. The priest must have read it quite slowly, for Francis (who certainly owned no missal) understood every word. Apparently he could understand Latin, although he wrote it poorly. I will quote the passage entirely and spare the reader the trouble of looking it up. Just a summary is not enough. Jesus is sending out his disciples:

"Preach as you go, saying, 'The kingdom of heaven is at hand.' Heal the sick, raise the dead, cleanse lepers, cast out demons. You received without pay, give without pay. Take no gold, nor silver, nor copper in your belts, nor bag for your journey, nor two tunics, nor sandals, nor a staff; for the laborer deserves his food. And whatever town or village you enter, find out who is worthy in it, and stay with him until you depart. As you enter the house, salute it. And if the house is worthy, let your peace come upon it; but if it is not worthy, let your peace return to you. And if anyone will not receive you or listen to your words, shake off the dust from your feet as you leave that house or town. Truly, I say to you, it shall be more tolerable on the day of judgment for the land of Sodom and Gomorrah than for that town.

"Behold, I send you out as sheep in the midst of wolves; so be wise as serpents and innocent as doves. Beware of men; for they will deliver you up to councils, and flog you in their synagogues, and you will be dragged before governors and kings for my sake, to bear testimony before them and the Gentiles. When they deliver you up, do not be anxious how you are to speak or what you are to say; for what you are to say will be given to you in that hour; for it is not you who speak, but the Spirit of your Father speaking through you."

Undoubtedly Francis had heard this Gospel before, but when he heard it this time it was as if scales suddenly fell from his eyes. He was like a person beside himself. Hardly was the Mass over when he begged the priest to read the Gospel to him once more and explain it. The priest did so. Recent investigators believe him to have been a Waldensian. In any event it is certain that the Waldensians regarded this passage of Holy Scripture with partiality since it called for a "life according to the gospel." It is also certain that exactly for this reason their greeting was "Peace be with you." Thirdly, it is certain that in the youth of Francis Bernardone a Waldensian was mayor of Assisi. The determined insistence of earlier biographers that Francis knew nothing of the Waldensians, and that no connection existed between him and this revival movement, cannot be maintained. Nevertheless, it remains true that there is nowhere the slightest indication that Francis at any point considered leaving the Church, even though Church authorities made so many difficulties for him.

But to return to the happening at Portiuncula. At one stroke the quest that had overshadowed him like a dark cloud since Spoleto ended. "That's what I want! That is what I am looking for! With my whole heart I long to do that!" And immediately he translated it into action. Hitherto he still dressed as his friend in Gubbio had fitted him out: tunic, leather belt, staff, traveling bag, shoes. Now he put all that aside, made for himself a shabby, coarse garment, took a rope for a belt, and the outfit was complete. Not satisfied with that, he began to preach in the open and in the church with the permission of the Bishop. "The Lord give you peace," was his greeting to all the world. In brief, he had found his way of life. That must also have struck others in the same manner. Even his biographer, Thomas of Celano, said he seemed to be completely different than before. At first people had simply regarded him as a madman – like his father did. Later they no longer molested him, but they still smiled pityingly. Now suddenly the tide turned and others began to join him.

The first was Bernard da Quintavalle, a prudent and respected merchant. He told Francis he wanted to dispose of everything the Lord had given him in whatever way Francis thought best. "Early tomorrow we will go to the church," said Francis, "and from the *gospel book* hear what the Lord has ordered his disciples to do." The following day they went with still a third, Peter Catani, a lawyer, to the church of St. Nicholas by the marketplace (today it is a police barracks). The gospel book lay alongside the altar so that anyone who wanted to could read it. (That was in the year 1209 [1208]!)

"Where shall we open it?" they said. Even Peter Catani, although he had studied at the famous University of Bologna, did not know his way around in Scripture; for only since the 1967 Synod has the Catholic Church been making an effort to bring canon law into harmony with Sacred Scripture! So Francis prayed to God that he might make known his will in the opening of the book. They opened it three times, hitting upon Matthew 19,21; Luke 9,3; and Matthew 16,24. They read there: "If you would be perfect, go, sell what you possess and give it to the poor." Then: "Take nothing for your journey, no staff, nor bag, nor bread, nor money." And finally: "If any man would come after me, let him deny himself and take up his cross and follow me." Then Francis cried out passionately: "Brothers, that is our life, that is our rule – for us and for all who wish to join us."

Now certainly much that is legendary may be coming into play here. The sources are not in complete agreement about it. I repeat the story because it demonstrates in any case that for Francis the experience of Portiuncula was not simply a narration that incidentally came from Holy Scripture. For him it comprised in a real way the revelation of his whole way of life, the end of his time of searching, the fulfillment of the promise of Spoleto. Holy Scripture as the word of God had consciously become his guide. For that reason, from this time on he will always say that he and his companions want to lead "a life according to the gospel." This consciousness was so strong in him that he disarmed all opponents with it and fought desperately to keep Scripture as the sole norm of his community. One cannot say that this only gradually took hold of him in later years, because that does not fit the facts.

The break is completely clear. *Before* Portiuncula there were dreams, visions, certain experiences, counsel from the Bishop, brief respites of prayer, which allowed Francis to grow slowly and painfully without giving him full clarity about what God really wanted of him. *After* Portiuncula it is all of a sudden completely clear: his mission consists of "a life according to the gospel." Disciples join him right away. They also take up a life according to the gospel. This decides everything else. Even in his *Testament,* which he wrote shortly before his death, we read: "When God gave me some friars, there was no one to tell me what I should do; but the Most High himself made it clear to me that I must live the life of the gospel."

That "there was no one to tell me what I should do," is noteworthy. It calls to mind two things in particular that bear mentioning here.

Before the Portiuncula event, Francis in his need turned to Bishop Guido, who was for him the competent representative of the official Church. But Guido did not show him what he should do. That was not only prudent, it was also religiously correct. The Bishop saw clearly that this young man was under the special guidance of God. He took care not to interfere disrespectfully. His job as chief shepherd consisted in this case only in guarding Francis against possible clearcut deviations which he might have fallen into, and in encouraging him to follow the call of God unswervingly. It is clear from the extant biographies that there were moments of doubt and discouragement, moments when he was tempted to give up his unusual way of life. One thinks, for instance, of the encounter with the pious old woman which made Francis ask himself if he really wanted to become like that. The Bishop was obviously surprised after the Portiuncula event, and to this very worldly man the ideas of his protégé did not seem very realizable – especially when they started to spread to more people. He certainly was informed about the Waldensians. One could have expected that he would feel obligated to lay down a veto because of the "dubiousness" of such a way; for the latter could end up in conflict with the Church and in "pernicious" errors (Manicheism, for instance). But the Bishop did not do that at all. Indeed he even granted Francis permission to preach. But he did not show him the way.

The second thing that comes to mind is this. The priest in Portiuncula may have been a Waldensian. But it was not he who pointed out the way to Francis either. He may have read the Biblical passage, but he must certainly not have added the slightest propaganda for his movement. Otherwise Francis could not have said so unaffectedly on his deathbed that nobody told him what to do. He really had been referred to Holy Scripture alone, and relied on it alone.

A year later the community of brothers already numbered twelve. In the meantime the directive to rebuild "my church," which Francis had received at San Damiano, became clear to him in the light of the gospel. "My church" was not a wayside chapel. It was the Church of Christ, his institution. It was in ruins, full of rents and tears, no longer dispensing life. Why? We will speak more of that later. Here the outlook of the young man is enough: The gospel no longer counted. In general, Francis did not have a problem with the question: What does the gospel *mean?* Thus he was all the more taken up with another question: Why was the gospel no longer operative and effective? People did not *live* according to the gospel! That was the sad state of affairs that things had come to. And the way to combat the situation was just as direct and simple: somebody must begin to do that again. Simply, straightforwardly, without sophistry, without adding or substracting anything, someone had to *live the gospel* and nothing else. That is what rebuilding the Church meant, that was Francis' mission. It was not just a personal mission but also a universal one.

The genius of Francis, it seems to me, lies in his courage to tackle things in a self-evident and simple way. The genius and the simplifier are close to one another. At first glance they are not distinguishable. Yet at the same time there is the sharpest possible difference between them, for the genius ascertains that the "self-evident" fundamentals no longer hold. Nobody will believe it, for everyone is convinced that the fundamentals do of course hold. When difficulties crop up, they improve one thing or another and get all tied up in extremely complicated and ingeniously worked-out corrective measures. Ultimately they wonder why their enormous expenditure of clever thought, and maybe even of material resources, does not bring the desired result.

That was exactly the situation in the Church at that time. It was a period of radical change and upheaval, in many respects comparable to the situation today. In the realm of church structure this showed up in all sorts of movements for reform. They began with the "Gregorian Reform," which originated with the popes appointed by Henry III (two hundred years before Francis) and reached its high point in Gregory VII (1073–1085). It would be an oversimplification to see in this only a power struggle between emperor and pope. On the whole one can say that during the first centuries after the year one thousand, the West left the stage of a primitive, unified culture and moved on to greater differentiation and more lively reflection. But the basic thrust of this process was thoroughly religious. More than a few popes took an active part as sincere reformers.

Among them was Innocent III (1198–1216), whom Francis now met. This youthful pope, who was only thirty-seven at the time of his accession, has often been called the most powerful pope in the entire history of the Church. This has led people to see in him a man with only power on his mind, one for whom religion represented merely a means to an end and who had no real religious thought. But that cannot be said in such an unequivocal manner. On the other hand, a person would have to be blind to deny that Lotario di Segni took delight in power. The game of politics was his life's blood. A former student of Paris and Bologna, he had not only a clever head but was perhaps the best lawyer of his time. He was called *pater iuris* ("father of law"). It was not just that he knew how to argue with theological acuity and elegance. The little man with piercing eyes and always dignified manner loved the political game. Like so many people of very acute intelligence, however, he lacked warmth of heart, the spontaneity of a kindly father. That explains why a Greek contemporary could say he was not Peter's successor but Constantine's, and why Will Durant could say in his great history of civilization that he was a Stoic rather than a Christian.

Still, the other side of his character should not be forgotten. Before he was pope had he not written *De contemptu mundi (On Contempt for the World),* in which he profoundly and impressively depicted the vanity of all earthly things? In contrast to his predecessors did he not meet the growing poverty movement halfway, insofar as the faith permitted? It is true, of course, that in doing so he had more bad experiences than good ones. Personally, however, he lived simply and austerely. And he did not shrink at challenging the fifteen hundred Council Fathers of Lateran IV (1215) with a welcoming speech which left nothing to be desired by those anxious for reform: "Widespread corruption in the spiritual realm is your most important concern. From here stems the evil of Christianity: faith wanes, religion becomes deformed...."

Hence one cannot turn the encounter between Francis and Innocent into a theatrical scene, complete with fireworks, and entitle it: "Two Worlds Meet." It is false to describe Francis as fundamentally a pacifist, although many of his words and actions taken by themselves can be interpreted that way. By the same token it is misleading to present Innocent as a cold, calculating powermonger, even if many of his actions could point in that direction. Such oversimplifications serve no one. Their consequence is that people put forward challenges for the present day which sound radical and promise great miracles, but turn out to be nothing but theatrical gimmicks. Such, for example, is the story of Francis' first papal visit which historical research has long since shown to be grotesque exaggeration. According to this story, Innocent III is supposed to have told the shabby Francis at his first papal visit: "Brother, go find the swine! You are better suited for them than for men. Wallow with them in the muck. Give them the rule you have composed and try your preaching on them!" Such also is the following comment: "So brutish were the Pope and the Curia that they were receptive only to sensual impressions." And such is the follow-up conclusion that Paul VI must now make up for the opportunity that Innocent III missed, that he must bring about a "total revolution and transform the Church into a Franciscan one" if he wants to be a "real" Holy Father (See Karl Ipser, *Franziskus: Der himmlische Kommunist,* 1967). Such theatrical gimmicks have yet to reform the Church.

But that other scene – depicted so frequently and impressively in paintings – also seems to me to obscure the true situation in an ominous way. It gives an account of a dream the Pope had in which the Church seemed to be tottering and collapsing. Along came an unlikely little man, who pressed his shoulders against the falling walls and set the building up again. The Pope woke up astonished and did not know how to interpret his dream. However, when he caught sight of Giovanni Bernardone – nicknamed Francesco – he recognized the features of the man in the dream and allowed his order. This story is edifying and beautiful. It fits well with the experience in San Damiano. It graphically portrays the importance of the Franciscan movement. That is all true.

Nevertheless it is improbable. For a dream interpreted by the Pope as revelation would have led to official confirmation of the rule, not just acquiescence. Aside from that, Innocent III does not seem to have been a man inclined to put much faith in dreams and visions. As we already pointed out, he evinced a style of thinking which in its temperateness one might have believed to be borrowed from the Stoics. And in general the circle from which he stemmed was the matrix of that strange "pre-Renaissance" carried out by his pupil Frederick II, who was later to become emperor. In any case, all this was swept up in the Gothic movement. However, common to the Pope and to his protégé and later opponent was a certain horror of all that tended to superstition, fanaticism, spiritual excess. During the Fourth Lateran Council (1215) he objected sharply to the sale of false relics and to the "foolish and unnecessary indulgences which certain prelates... are not ashamed to grant. By them they make the keys of the Church ridiculous and rob penances of their validity." Similarly Frederick II abolished the ordeal and duelling as a legal process. This spirit of sobriety, which was far ahead of its time, even impressed Pope John XXIII. In his *Journal of a Soul* we find a special reference to Innocent III, whom Roncalli, now pope and already past eighty, pulls out "again" and finds "so rich in pastoral teaching." How much Pope John, in contrast with Pius XII, treated with suspicion everything that smacked of wonder-seeking, be it devotions or pious "movements," is well known. Besides, it is established that the dream story was introduced relatively late. It may therefore have value as legend in the strict sense of the word. That is to say, it describes a situation appropriately. But it is not history.

A third version of the meeting between Francis and Innocent sounds more likely. According to this version, through the mediation of Bishop Guido of Assisi, the Benedictine Cardinal John Colonna, whom Innoncent had appointed Bishop of Sabina, was the first to deal with the twelve begging friars. It was some time before he had convinced himself of the purity of their intentions. This is understandable in the light of the reform movements springing up in those days, in which all sorts of spiritual and very unspiritual, orthodox and heterodox, thought-out and emotional tendencies were mixed.

But then he interceded with the Pope for Francis. And his friendship with Innocent as well as his good reputation with the cardinals – he was regarded as a leader of the reform party – became a bulwark for the young community. The argument which he offered is worth close attention. He is supposed to have said to the Pope: "I have found a very perfect man who wants to *live by the words of the holy gospel* and to observe *evangelical perfection in all things.* It seems to me the Lord will renew the faith of the holy Church in the whole world through him." The core of the statement is obviously that Francis wants to live according to the gospel.

Then the Pope allowed the friars from Assisi to come to him. Francis submitted his program. This first rule has been lost, and all attempts to reconstruct it are of dubious value. However, one thing is certain – that it was not a "rule" in the sense of the rules of other orders, but a compilation of passages from Sacred Scripture. No further interpretation was to be provided. Nothing was to be subtracted. Nothing was to be added. That must have seemed revolutionary, for with it what all orders held as essential *fell away:* namely, that even if individuals possessed nothing, the community must have property. His rule also dropped the notion of these friars living together in a fixed cloister. The "holy" world of order members as a segregated community alongside the profane world of men seemed dissolved. That must have appeared somewhat naïve and unrealistic to the Pope, and for that reason he rated this "rule" as entirely too strict. "You must also think of those who will come after you and perhaps not have the same enthusiasm." Here again Francis resisted, even as he had the Cardinal earlier. He knew that any giving-in would have led in essence to accepting the rule of one of the already-existing orders. And that was exactly what he did not want. Not at any price!

Consider the Cistercians, for example. What an impetus to renewal they represented in the Church! How quickly they slid back again through the riches of their monasteries! St. Bernard died in the year 1153. Thanks to him, the Cistercians, a reform branch of the Benedictines which began in 1098, went through a fabulous period of growth. In the space of twenty years the number of monasteries rose from thirty to three hundred and forty-three. About the year thirteen hundred there were supposed to have been sixty thousand Cistercian monks in six hundred and thirty-nine monasteries. Although the rule strictly obliged extreme renunciation and simplicity, only four years after Bernard's death the monks in his monastery at Clairvaux did not want to do manual labor; so they bought Saracen slaves for themselves. And because of their collective wealth they scarcely had a good reputation among the laity. There is the well-known reply of Richard the Lionheart to the priest, Fulk of Neuilly, who was exhorting people to join the Crusades. "You wish me to repudiate my three daughters: Arrogance, Greed, and Unchastity. I bequeath them to those who deserve them most: my Arrogance to the Templars; my Greed to the monks of Cîteaux; my Unchastity to the clergy."

The statement must have occurred around the year 1200, when Francis was a youth. Both Innocent and Francis knew only too well the situation it describes. It led Innocent to the conclusion

Picture page 73:
Francis had preached the word of the Lord in Ancona. He then moved on. In the vicinity of Osimo he and Brother Paolo came across a shepherd who was grazing a herd of billy-goats and she-goats. A shy little lamb scampered alongside, grazing peacefully. Francis came to a standstill. Overcome by compassion he said to Paolo: "Do you see how tamely the lamb conduct itself among the billy-goats and she-goats? That is how our Lord conducted himself among the Pharisees and priestly officials. Come, let us buy the little lamb, so that we can liberate it from this community." They had no money, nothing in fact, but a passing merchant bought the little lamb for them. Afterwards they gave it to Clare's community in San Severino. The community tended the lamb for a long time, and they wove a habit for Francis out of its wool. Francis received the cowl just before a general chapter of the order. With "great joy of spirit" he accepted the gift and asked everyone to rejoice with him.

Picture pages 74–75:
On one occasion Francis noticed that a sick brother (the priest Sylvester) longed for grapes but did not dare to ask for them. Without further ado Francis headed off to the vineyard with him. Seating himself and his companion alongside a grapevine, Francis began to eat grapes with him, "so that the brother would not be ashamed at eating alone."

Picture pages 76–77:
Francis customarily spent all of Lent in solitude. So on Shrove Tuesday in 1211 he found himself on the shore of Lake Trasimeno (see photo). He knew a man there who was devoted to him. He asked this man to row him out to a completely uninhabited island, and to do it that night so he would not be noticed by anyone. Francis took only two small loaves of bread with him. He found shelter and secrecy in a thick hedge where the animals had cleared a kind of campsite. On Holy Thursday his friend came and brought him back. Francis had eaten half a loaf of bread so that he would not become conceited about his fasting.

Picture page 78:
View of Assisi. As the dying Francis was being transported to the Portiuncula, which was situated outside the town, he bade the litter-bearers to set him down. With his gaze directed towards Assisi, he blessed the town he loved so much: "May God bless you, holy town, so that many souls are saved by you. May many servants of God dwell in you, and may many of your inhabitants be chosen to enter the kingdom of eternal life."

that discipline had to be tightened and faith deepened. Francis opened the gospel and to him it was plain: the gospel had to be *lived*. He certainly knew well that it was also important to reform the education of priests and clerics. But unlike other reformers of his time he never thought of criticizing the training publicly. Here again the only help that he wanted to offer was simply living the gospel.

The Pope dismissed the strange evangelist without making a decision. He called a consistory, that is, an extraordinary assembly of cardinals. It had a wholly different and decisive import in those days, an import that we would call "collegial" today. The Pope presented the case. At first the cardinals reacted negatively, as was to be expected. Too many reform communities already haunted the scene. Five years later, Lateran IV (1215) would forbid the founding of new religious orders! Even Dominic had to submit to this and accept the rule of the Augustinian canons. But in this consistory Cardinal Colonna, the first in that line of proud Colonnas who would follow, stood up and said: "Venerable Brothers, this man desires only that we allow him to *live according to the gospel*. If we explain that this surpasses human strength, then we are maintaining that it is impossible to follow the gospel. By that we mock Christ, the author of the gospel." His speech silenced the opposition.

The Pope summoned Francis and the friars to him once more. This time Francis told a fairy tale. He was able to express himself in that style far better than in abstract concepts. "Once there lived in a desert place a very beautiful but very poor woman. The king of the realm saw her, and she found favor in his eyes. He desired to marry her in the belief that she would bear him beautiful children. When the marriage was entered into and consummated, the woman bore many sons. And she began to wonder to herself and say, 'What shall I, a poor woman, do with all the children I have had? I have no property on which they can live!' So she said to her sons, 'Do not be afraid, for you are the children of a king. Go to his court and he will give you everything that you need!' But when they had come to the king, he marveled at their beauty and saw that they were like him. He said to them, 'Whose sons are you?' They replied they were the sons of the poor woman who lived in the desert. Then the king embraced them and said, 'Fear not, for you are my children! I feed so many strangers at my table, how much more will I feed you who are my lawful sons!' And he sent to the woman in the desert saying she should send all her children to him at the palace, so that he could support them!"

That was the tale. Francis immediately added the meaning. He cried, "Lord Pope!" (One still addressed the pope simply in those days.) "That poor woman in the desert is I. God in his mercy has looked upon me. I have borne him sons in Christ. And the King of Kings has told me that he will provide for my offspring; for if he supports every stranger, it befits him all the more to provide for the children of his own household. God gives earthly goods to sinners because of the love which they have for their children; how abundantly will he pour out his gifts on those who follow *his gospel* and to whom he is therefore under obligation!" On the strength of that the Pope orally sanctioned the life of the first Friars Minor. That was enough in any event to assure that at the Fourth Lateran Council no other rule was imposed upon the Franciscans, "an already established and approved Order."

Now how much of this version is history and how much is pious embroidery we do not know. But what is clear is this: Francis wanted to live the gospel, and because he wanted that his plan was approved.

4. Poverty: The Future of the Church

Many of the people who today regard Francis as the ideal image of the saint of the future are inclined to do so, directly or indirectly, because they see him as a social reformer. They readily point to the covenant made in 1210 between the noblemen (the *Maiores*) and the middle-class people (the *Minores*) in the town of Assisi, which brought a long-standing feud to an end. In return for a modest ground-rent, the nobleman renounced his feudal rights. The inhabitants of the villages belonging to Assisi were put on an equal footing with the townspeople, and serfs were freed. Amnesty was granted to those banished for political reasons. This covenant, of which we still have the official record, became the Magna Carta of Assisi.

This document undoubtedly bears witness to the upheaval that was taking place in that era, this upheaval being a side-effect of the Crusades. On the one hand the Crusades brought about widespread unification of Europe's countries and peoples. Now more than ever before they formed an empire, and a movement which arose in one area readily spread to other areas. At the same time, however, the spices and luxuries of the Orient stimulated new cravings. As the American Franciscan James Meyer pointed out, "the Crusades had opened the eyes of Europe to a new world of creature comforts, with a result comparable as a whole in its social effect to the bedazzlement we moderns are experiencing in these latter decades what with the auto, the radio, the cinema, aviation, and the like" (*Social Ideals of St. Francis*, 2nd rev. edn., St. Louis and London, 1948, p. 22). Trade and commerce took an astounding upturn, and in its wake the monetary system became a dominant force. The result was sharp opposition between the *nouveaux riches* and the old nobility.

Another result was a radical shift in outlook. Up until that time a person had to win a power base in order to become wealthy. That meant ownership of land, the exercise of authority on a smaller or larger scale. Wealth was merely a function of power. Now, however, a person could be rich without possessing any power base in land ownership. The symbol of this was money. It shattered a whole social structure by tearing itself loose from the old structures and making itself autonomous. To those tied down to the old order it must have seemed like a cancerous growth. Money did not seem to fit into this traditional order. Thus it became the symbol of detachment from any and every order, including the moral order. People saw the lurking danger of licentiousness and the denigration of all traditional values, for no one could really picture a new social order in which money would have a recognized place and value.

A social reformer would certainly have felt obliged to propose such a plan, or at least the broad outlines of it. But Francis of Assisi had no such thought, and he never made the slightest efforts in this direction. We do not know whether he was even a party to the Assisi covenant of 1210. In any case, the covenant itself seems to have been prompted by the critical situation in which Assisi found itself under pressure from Perugia. Defeated militarily and bereft of resources, Assisi could not afford bloody disputes among its citizenry. All the citizens would have to stand together if their town was to resist successfully the overweening adversary. Not the preaching of Francis but the critical situation of Assisi appears to have been the driving force behind the covenant of 1210. Here, as in many other cases, pious historiography has tried to attribute every happy outcome to the impact of the Church or her saints. This tack not only distorts the proper perspectives but also places practically insurmountable obstacles in our way when we are trying to grasp the real meaning and significance of the saints. It has drained the Church and the saints of their potency and hindered their fertility.

But the background of events, which I have briefly mentioned above, is very important if we are to understand why the *Poverello* had such a hate-complex with regard to money – a hatred that never left him. Although he certainly knew how to handle money in his early days, as the story of his conversion shows, he later chose to have nothing to do with it at all. His companions were never to accept money when they begged or worked, not even to help others. To Francis money was so much dirt on the road, and in drastic ways he tried to transmit his outlook to the members of the Franciscan community. Francis would have been spared many painful and brutal experiences if he had not nurtured such bitter enmity towards money.

So we are compelled to ask where this enmity came from. It is useless to try to trace it back to rational grounds. Francis was a man of intuition and spontaneous feeling who had a fine feel for the concrete situation. We may talk a great deal today about reading the signs of the time in the light of faith, but that is scarcely a new injunction for Christians. It has always been there. But the signs take on special importance in a time of change, whereas they may attract little or no attention in epochs that flow by like a calm, undisturbed stream. Now the dawning thirteenth century was a time of upheaval. And perhaps one can simply say that a man with a strong religious sense intuitively perceived this radical change in money itself. For him money became the symbol for a whole aggregate of many diverse changes. A scholarly observer, in our sense of the word, would not have seen the forest for the trees as he went about analyzing all the individual elements involved. For all his keenness and exactness, he would have left himself and his readers in the dark. The peculiar genius of the prophet, on the other hand, lies precisely in the fact that he can capture a whole epoch in a concrete concept which he has grasped intuitively.

Now my feeling is that one can unhesitatingly describe Francis as a real prophet, precisely because he signalized money as the menacing power of a new era that was dawning. In his well known book, *Die Antwort der Mönche* (1968), Walter Dirks is of the opinion that Francis caught the scent of capitalism itself – not capitalism as an economic system, but capitalism as a "motive force of man's soul." His love of poverty was a challenge hurled against the spirit of money, because the real danger lay in the *humaneness* of the new wealth. It was not a "moral" danger in the usual sense because the moral qualities of the merchant class would mark them off from the unbridled nobility for centuries. It was their *heart* that was compromised and jeopardized: "The secularization of succeeding centuries would proceed from the middle class, and its uprightness would serve to justify the apostasy." In the middle-class mode of life people will find "a very humane form of existence without God."

I believe that there is more than a little truth in Dirks's brilliant explanation and interpretation. It may well be incontestable that neither the world nor the Church has managed to cope with the "spirit of money" as yet. And one can indeed trace the line of association back to the early eras of primitive capitalism. But that is not the whole story at all, because the significance of money has changed radically. It has become an indispensable component of our overall economic life. Even the poorest person cannot live without money, and it has completely lost any taint of being ill-gotten gain. In particular, the connotation of luxury has now disappeared from it completely. Today money is much more the embodiment of stability, peace, and order than the embodiment of upheaval and revolution which it was in the time of Francis. Perhaps Walter Dirks would agree with all that too, and I should like to think he does. Money is the symbolic embodiment of world security. In Francis' day that was something new. Later on it became the normal state of affairs. Today it has become a token of world manipulability. In any case it bespeaks the loss of direct reference to God. The whole problem of the self-made world surfaces here.

Now it may well be that Francis sensed the threat posed by money in terms of secularization. He was a rich young man to begin with, even though he never used money as a means to become richer. Even then he found it more or less contemptible. But he did use it as a *means:* to win prestige, votaries, and other social aims. That changed when his outlook changed. He then began to use it for pious purposes, which led to very unpleasant altercations with his father. And he also saw how money matters could lead people to act in very unchristian ways, not excluding his own bishop. All that could well have produced an antimoney complex in him. There is no denying that. But it would have been wholly out of character for the Poverello to act and live out of a sense of nay-saying or anxiety or hatred. The qualities that have made him so attractive to every generation since then run directly counter to that. Pope John XXIII, who was much like Francis in this respect, would never have ranked him among the "prophets of doom" whom he criticized at the opening of Vatican II. Francis was not one of those well-intentioned advisers who are off on the wrong track.

Francis was a positive-oriented person to his very core. He took the victory of good for granted. He knew nothing of the attitude of "grave concern" that is evinced by many judicious and important men today, who are led to sound warnings on every side and to raise defensive barricades. So I find it hard to believe that the poverty of St. Francis, which stands out as his most conspicuous trait, arose from his sensing or recognizing the "danger" of secularization. If this explanation were true, then his poverty would have had some traces of defensiveness and melancholy in it. It might still appear remarkable to us but there would also be a touch of horror in it, even as there is in the castle of San Angelo in Rome which symbolizes the last refuge of the pope.

It is true that many interpreters of St. Francis, reacting violently against the maudlin nature-lover which many pious souls turned him into, stress the harshness of his poverty to such a degree that it does really seem to be a protective wall erected out of anxiety. Now it is all well and good to react against the maudlin sentimentality and to underline the surprising harshness of Francis' primitive poverty. But it is wrong to catalog it as a defensive armament or something donned for show. Francis did not love poverty as the astronaut loves his space suit or as the medieval knight loved his clumsy armor. He loved poverty because a "life without possessions" seemed more desirable than a life with personal property and possessions. And his reasoning was not based on the advice of Pope Gregory the Great, who maintained that a man should go naked to wrestle with the devil so that the latter would have nothing to get a hold on.

For Francis of Assisi poverty was *a matter of style.* He loved poverty because with it he could show God that he trusted him unreservedly. Even more, he loved poverty because he could show other human beings how much trust he had in their goodness. His motto was not the one which the fascists plastered all over Italy (i. e., "live dangerously"), only to show that they were all too human and hence not up to it when it came down to death. Francis was motivated by something else, by a profoundly personal and existential union with God and his fellow men. That is why he was so happy when he heard the words of the Gospel telling Christ's disciples to go out without staff or purse and to eat what others put before them. "That is what I have been looking for," he exclaimed. That is why he did not repudiate *work* either, but rather put it in first place: because it signified useful service to others. That is why he was delighted when he could help others with gifts and make them happy, and why he did not garnish his gift-giving with admonitions about "proper use." In his "living without possessions," as he described it, he daily and hourly came to know both *God* and his *neighbors* in terms of their most appealing and sympathetic side. Through the commitment of his whole personality he demonstrated to them *his trust in their liberality.*

A second aspect came into the picture here, one which is obvious to a human being of today: through such a life Francis showed himself to be *credible.* We often overlook the fact that the whole thought of Francis was what we today would call "missionary oriented." He was deeply conscious of a "mission," of a unique mission that distinguished him from everyone else. That is why he could be so upset when ecclesiastical authorities tried to impose on him the rule of some already existing religious order. He certainly had nothing against the older orders; we can find no trace of a polemic against them. But his mandate was a special one that did not dovetail with the pathway taken by others.

Thus we cannot rest content with describing Franciscan poverty in the general terms that are often used: e. g., as *being free* for God. Francis was acquainted with this interpretation, to be sure, and used it to good advantage on occasion. Consider, for example, his famous reply to the Bishop of Assisi. But that was not the core of his love of poverty. That was not the distinctive character of his way. That was not the radiant charm which somehow continues to play around Franciscan poverty even today. I should like to suggest that the core of Franciscan poverty lay in the direct challenge posed to God; in the appeal to his magnanimity which was authorized by the Gospel itself and which was therefore a striking proof of credibility; in what was at bottom a deeply rooted personal conviction.

That explains why Francis loved to cite the story of the sheep and the wolves. For it suggests that the Christian as Christian, i. e., as the witness to God's message, cannot ground himself on any sort of human security.

Also in line with this is the peculiar reserve that Francis displayed towards the budding scholarly science of his day. It was not his business to devote himself to theoretical ideas and conceptual abstractions. In this sense he was quite obviously not a speculative theologian. The strangest stories are told about his antipathy towards theological science. It is not that he criticized or denigrated theology as such, that he wrote it off as vacuous conceptual game-playing. On the contrary, he could speak quite highly of it. But he did take the most drastic measures to keep his followers far away from scholarly science. It led to bitter disputes which played no small part in his resignation as head of the Order. But he held fast to his opinion right up until his death.

It is not easy to uncover the underlying motives for his attitude, even though much has been written about it. It seems to me that Francis' attitude towards scholarly knowledge can only be viewed in connection with his attitude towards money; I do not think anyone will deny that. It is the same inner attitude and the same personal experience that is operative: i. e., his experience of Christ. Perhaps that is not quite correct either. It might be more correct to say: his experience of God.

In this respect Francis is extremely modern. For, the human being and Christian of today wants to be able to experience God, to meet him in an authentic encounter. He is not happy with some "God above us" whom we lay hold of in unintelligible concepts, whom we talk about in pale "theological" abstractions and then project back into our practical life. At best such abstractions have schooled the mind in olympian acrobatics.

What is entailed here is a fully human way of knowing God, one more akin to the Biblical sense of "knowing" and hence inseparable from real life. Like Karl Rahner one can hope and expect that the piety of the future will be mystagogic – so long as the term is not misunderstood. It does not refer, at least in the first instance, to mystical experience as a strictly supernatural intervention by God to which some individuals may be specifically called. It refers instead to a presentiment of nearness that lays hold of the whole man and ushers him into the ultimate reality, a reality which reveals itself as a Thou. Today we look for it first of all in other human beings, in selfless surrender to them; and that seems to correspond very well with the mystery of the Incarnation.

When I was reading the texts that reveal Francis' inner depths, I was astonished to note how deeply his piety was Theocentric rather than Christocentric. Even in the apparition which imprinted the stigmata on his body, we cannot be sure whether the blazing figure of light is supposed to represent Christ or merely an angelic messenger. For Francis, Christ is a gateway. The core is the Father, the primal ground of all things. The man from Umbria is imbued with a cosmic consciousness. It gives soaring wings to his "Canticle of Brother Sun" even though it may not rank as exceptional in literary terms. Through Francis' way of looking at things, all natural realities – sun, moon, water, fire, earth, and flower – get and keep their own personal note. They are seen as gifts, as messengers. It is not just that they are meant to convey a message; rather they *are* a message by their very existence. That is why he calls them "Brothers" and "Sisters." He experiences them as deriving from the same Father, and there is something of their Father in them. They represent the Father's address to him, and his reply to them is a reply to the Father. Now one may certainly say that this is an oversimplification, but that does not erase the deeper core imbedded in it. There is no trace of maudlin sentimentality, no trace of the pantheism that many would like to read into Francis. Yet the cosmology of the Poverello evinces a clear "yes" to the world that can scarcely be matched. In a wholly simple and unpretentious way he actually experiences God in the world of nature and in his encounters with human beings.

If Francis of Assisi had read or heard of Teilhard de Chardin's *Mass on the World,* he would have concurred gleefully with its sentiments even though the evolutionary ideas of the modern scientist might have seemed quite strange to him. He would have had no trouble in affirming the kernel of this thought to be a reality which he had experienced. By contrast, such an experience is blocked off from many people in our day by a welter of methodological and scientific questions – even though these questions do have their rightful place.

The fruitfulness of his understanding of God and the world was something which Francis experienced day after day in his songs and sermons. No one could dispute them. It was not only simple folk who were overpowerd by them. Even educated people, those in Bologna for example, were evidently impressed by his spontaneous insight and vision. It is not noted often enough that the vast majority of his early disciples and companions were educated men rather than "primitive" spirits.

In his multivolume history of civilization, Will Durant dates *The Age of Faith* (volume IV) from Constantine to Dante (325–1300). He is surely right in saying that the high point of the age of faith contained the seeds of the subsequent age of reason. The rise of the latter age was not due solely to the flood of translations from Arabic and Greek that now inundated the western world. Nor was it due solely to the growing store of *leisure time* (Lat. *schola*) and prosperity that abetted the rise of schools. Rather, these were preconditions and attendant circumstances which were required for such a new beginning and which modified the end result. But far more basic was the fact that the age of faith had reached a borderline-limit. It had gone as far and as high as it could go within the framework of a specified culture and mode of thought. This fact is concretely evident in such figures as Joachim of Fiore, Francis, and Dante who are intimately connected. At the same time, however, it was already flowing over into a visionary future that broke down the old categories. At this point the purest fruits of the age of faith and the first initiatives of the age of reason are still at one. They would separate from each other as they proceeded farther along the new pathway. Reason would step forth as the antipole to faith, and sometimes as its enemy. With the dissolution of the old forms, the old faith which animated them would be cast aside.

This process was already visible in Francis' time. Right nearby was Bologna, the most famous university in the West at that time. It did not have a theological faculty, but it of course had a faculty of law. Theology appeared to be jurisprudence – with a sharply anti-ecclesiastical tinge. Bernard of Clairvaux complained that the law of Justinian was on everyone's lips while no one wanted to hear of God's law any more. Next to law stood medicine; and it became a commonplace saying that two out of three doctors were atheists. The courtly world of Frederick II was taking shape during this same period. Excommunicated at one point, this brilliant rationalist was called the "wonder of the world" (*"stupor mundi"*) by his contemporaries.

A century earlier the rationalist Abelard (1079–1142) had taught in France. While he did not openly deny any dogma of the Faith, he called faith itself into question insofar as he believed one could and should prove everything. We modern Christians may find much to approve in Abelard. He seems to be correct when he says that those who advocate a faith without intelligible understanding "are often trying to conceal their own inability to teach the Faith in an intelligible way." And his words have a modern tone when he suggests that "hope" is the only advantage of the Christian vis-a-vis the Jew and the philosopher. Yet even the modern Christian shrinks back in dismay from Abelard's audacity in trying to unlock and resolve every mystery. For him there is no mystery at all. Students flocked to him even after he had left Paris. When he built a flimsy hermitage in a desolate area between Fontainebleau and Troyes, hundreds of students joined him there – sleeping on straw and rushes and eating oats and herbs. This state of affairs went on for three years. The age was intoxicated with reason.

Once again I should like to point out that it would be very one-sided to attribute this invasion of *reason* into the faith-dominated world of the earlier Middle Ages solely to the new-found acquaintance with Arabic philosophy. What is at work here is an *inner* process of growth, a developmental phase. The age sought to master the new complex of problems in two ways. One way might be called the baptism of Aristotle. Rational thinking was accorded its rights. It marked the first step along a road whose end was not foreseen. Indeed, at the start it was not evident at all because ingenious syntheses of faith and reason swept all before them. The awesome structure of scholastic theology took hold of the Church. Revelation provided the data, Aristotle provided the method for working on it. This method consisted of sober logical thinking, abstraction, and strictly rational combinations. In this sense theology was a scholarly science. But it had not undertaken the task of demonstrating the faith; it took the latter as its presupposition.

Thus two types of thought and knowledge were combined. In terms of their inner structure they were wholly different, but that does not mean that they necessarily had to contradict each other. However, it does raise some questions: Do they not presuppose psychic outlooks which cannot easily be maintained alongside each other in one and the same person? And what will happen if a whole epoch should be imbued with one or the other outlook? Could that not lead people into an atheistic age?

It is astonishing to note the agnosticism displayed by Thomas Aquinas when it comes to saying what we can utter about God with the aid of reason alone. To be sure, he maintains that we can prove the existence of God. What God is, however, wholly eludes our knowledge. In the *Summa theologica* he says: "Once we have established the existence of a thing, then we can go on to ask about its manner of existence in order to arrive at its essence. In the case of God, of course, we cannot know what he is; at best we can only know what he is not." In his commentary on the Epistle to the Romans, Thomas is even more pointed: "One thing remains wholly unknown in this present life; that is, what God is." Here Thomas is talking about man's effort to lay hold of God in a concept, which is in fact impossible.

But is spiritual knowledge possible only in concepts? Even in Holy Scripture we find God refusing to speak of himself in a "concept": "I am who I am" (Ex. 3,14). That is how he reveals himself to Moses. But there is more involved here. If a person should want to reduce the Faith to believed "truths" that can be captured in concepts, then it would be all too easy for him to overlook its most essential element. Here, it seems to me, is where Francis' intuitive fear of "theology" comes in.

Francis was a man who experienced God intuitively. His reform did not entail a demythologizing analysis based on reason. He did demythologize, to be sure, even as Holy Scripture had demythologized the polytheism of an earlier day. Francis demythologized the popular superstitions of his day; but his guiding standard was the gift of the "discernment of spirits," the concrete experience of the *authenticity* of his religious experiences. In matters of faith this was far surer for him than rational, scholarly knowledge. He felt it threatened and was in danger of succumbing to alienation.

I would suggest that his thrust here was the same thing that Ignatius of Loyola had in mind three hundred years later with the first method he chose in his *Spiritual Exercises.* He grounded his exercises wholly on this method, and he like Francis before him was misconstrued. The creation of Ignatius was turned into a military drill-exercise, while that of Francis was turned into a spiritualism that paid no heed to the reality of the world. In truth, however, Ignatius was looking for a methodology to attain knowledge of God's concrete will, a knowledge that could not be laid hold of in concepts or attained by reason, a knowledge that ultimately was grounded only on the unmistakable personal experience of authenticity which he rated superior to rational analysis. And Francis for his part passionately espoused that which was *most real* in reality and which he had experienced in his concrete life: the God who was concealed in all things and sustained all of reality. This reality could be experienced concretely by man, but Francis felt it – or better, *saw* it – jeopardized by the scholarly science he encountered. Both Ignatius and Francis were realists, and both were wholeheartedly concerned with the same non-rational knowledge.

In his reserved attitude towards scholarly knowledge Francis may well have seemed like a reactionary. Even many of his own followers did not understand him on this point. They turned away from him soon after his death and, with the blessing of the Church, sought to vie with the Dominicans in their eagerness to baptize scholarly science. In so doing, did they fail to understand the authentic mandate of the Franciscans?

For all their scholarly work, I think, the Franciscans have never really disowned the process of knowing the deeper knowledge of their founding father. They have never lost their homesickness for this deeper kind of knowledge. Bonaventure, the greatest Franciscan theologian, is said to have asked his contemporary Thomas Aquinas, the "sun" of Dominican scholarship, how he could pray to the *"ens a se"* ("being of itself"). God is not a philosophical conclusion but a living presence! Perhaps it is no accident that while the Dominican school came closer and closer to empty conceptual games – training admirable artists of the intellect, but more and more in the atmosphere of a carnival sideshow than in the atmosphere of concrete reality – the Franciscans became pioneers in the natural sciences. One need only think of Roger Bacon. It may also be no accident that the intellectual French evinced sympathetic feelings for the Dominicans, while the reality-oriented English evinced sympathy for the Franciscans. In any case the fact is that right up to today it is the Franciscan school, more than any other, that has devoted attention and effort to a *theologia cordis,* a "theology of the heart." However misleading and contradictory this term may seem, its orientation and goal is the spiritual talent of their founder, Francis, who thought it was more important to put new life into this talent than to baptize reason.

I recognize that these brief remarks are a bit overly subtle and pointed, but these pages do not and cannot propose to do more.

Indeed many readers may feel that they are a wholly unwarranted digression from the theme of this chapter. But that they certainly are not. A person will never understand the poverty of the Poverello, or be able to get a feel for it, if he simply casts a compassionate glance at his meager, threadbare habit. Even all the stories about his practice of poverty, which occasionally strike us as strange and bizarre, do not help here. One must make an effort to find the psychic and spiritual core of this unique man. From there everything falls into its proper place – almost effortlessly in my estimation. All the perspectives shift, the contradictory becomes a supporting buttress, and the bizarre becomes a jubilant and obvious certainty. It would be strange if it were missing.

Now an indispensable component of his psychic core was the way in which Francis knew and experienced God, the way in which he walked in God's company and felt at home. The rationalistic approach of the new scholarly disciplines may well have seemed a waste of time by comparison. And when he saw many of his followers, not the worst ones either, taking little libraries of scholarly books along on their missionary trips because they felt they could not otherwise "bring the gospel home" to their contemporaries, then his heart constricted with pain. "How awful!" he thought to himself. No, a thousand times no: that was not *his* way, the way God had shown him so that he might become the way for many others, the way he was to follow in restoring the dilapidated Church. The poverty which Francis wanted to teach his followers was a poverty that was not subject to rational vindication. Or, to put it more prudently, it was a poverty that is incomprehensible to us. We attribute it to his straightforward disposition. We usually glide over it quickly in biographies, or else we diffuse its efficacy with all sorts of distinctions: "That is not what was meant."

The learned Anthony of Padua is then brought into the picture. Formerly an Augustinian, he joined the friars while Francis was still alive. Francis had a curiously respectful relationship with him. He had nothing against the fact that Anthony accepted a professorship at the University of Bologna. An extant letter bears witness to this. The friendship between Francis and Dominic provides a further piece of evidence, even though we know very little about it. It does seem that Dominic admired Francis. He was present as an observer at one of the great Chapters of Assisi at least. He also took over from Francis the principle that not only the individual member but also the Order as a whole should not possess property. But we do not know to what extent Francis allowed his thought and activity to be influenced by Dominic. In the question of poverty at least, Dominic did not influence the thinking of Francis in any way, so far as I can see. The most one can say is that they never got into a serious quarrel over the issue. But that is not surprising because Francis never forced his ideas on others or presented them as the only correct ones for his age.

In this respect Francis is very different from many attempts at renewal in our own day. While I find them admirable, I am struck by the intolerance they display in proclaiming their way to be the only one, or at least the best one. Francis never did anything like that. He had his own way. He was convinced that God had pointed out this way to him. Hence he was very intolerant when anyone sought to put obstacles in his path. But he was quite ready to acknowledge other ways besides his own.

This proves, it seems to me, that he did not derive his approach from any ideology. Ideologies are always intolerant. They do not put up with any competing ideologies; indeed they cannot, because their existence would indicate a hole in their own system and hence its fragility. Francis did not live on the basis of an ideology. He lived on the basis of an inner experience, his own inner experience which he felt could be communicated as well. Full of hesitation and astonishment at first, he gradually came to communicate it in tones of jubilation and thankfulness. But he never forced it on people as the only possible experience.

Let us get back to the question of poverty, poverty with respect to scholarly knowledge, which Francis apparently demanded of his followers. When he returned from Africa he learned that his friars, emulating the Dominicans, had opened a house of studies in Bologna. He immediately gave it up, throwing out everyone in it including the sick. Houses of study! For Francis that seemed to be the beginning of the end. The whole argument with Brother Elias, who would later be called Elias of Cortona, can be traced back to this question.

My feeling is that this puzzle admits of only one solution: Francis possessed a knowledge about God that was based on his own living experience. So strong and radiant were the sparks it gave off that book knowledge seemed pale by comparison; book knowledge could not enrich him. So we are confronted with a paradox: Francis chooses to be poor in scholarly knowledge so that he will not lose his own rich treasury of knowledge. Francis experienced God in everything, above all in prayer. His prayer was not reflective contemplation of religious matters. Insofar as we know anything about it from the casual remarks of his closest companions, it was a direct dialogue of question and petition and answer, dealing with concrete issues and addressed personally to a Thou. He "wrestled" with God as Jacob had wrestled with the angel. It was the same sort of personal confrontation that the Bible describes variously in connection with Moses and the prophets.

It was easy for Francis to ascertain that Anthony's life was grounded on a very similar experience. He had not given up his comfortable life as a canon on the basis of scholarly considerations. He had been lured by a "call" that touched and stamped his whole person. I have only a fragmentary knowledge of the life of Anthony of Padua, but one need only look at his sermons to see that scholarly knowledge ever remained a mere tool and helpmate. It was not the driving force behind his preaching.

The same holds true for Francis. Francis hoped and expected to receive this support from his community. Now I realize how risky such an approach can be, even when a person imagines that he is sticking to Holy Scripture alone, and even when he submits to the judgment of the Church. But the fact is that this approach has never grown stagnant in the Church, not even in this "age of science" of which we justifiably boast. We shall speak more of that later.

Here we are still faced with another question: Does this "intellectual poverty," if we can call it that for a moment, have a relationship to the poverty in temporal possessions and its underlying motives just described, or are they two basic psychic attitudes that really have nothing in common?

I would suggest that they are connected with each other. If material poverty was rooted in a challenge to the generosity of God and one's fellow men, then it presupposed an incomparable trust in God. This trust was not empty talk or pious utterance, for it was followed by a supremely concrete leap into a life of insecurity. And it was not blind trust either. It was carried out with open and seeing eyes. Seeing what? It could only be God, not an abstract God but a God experienced in one's personal life. That brings us right back to the same fundamental experience we described in connection with Francis' intellectual poverty. They are two fruits of the same tree. They are not identical, of course. Indeed one might be inclined to ask here: If a person shoulders one of them, must he also flesh out the other in his life? I should like to answer "yes" to that question, even though I see very well that history does not concur with my answer. But must history be so pure and perfect? Is it not usually a compromise? And does there not always remain a yearning for the pure ideal?

Francis made a beginning, a beginning that was to be followed by others. He was not without efficacy in his own day, but it is true that he did not manage to develop his movement to its fullest. This is evident in the bitter struggles with the Spirituals. In part bolstered and in part falsified by the Joachimites and their grandiose visions of the future, a portion of Franciscan poverty seemed to end up as a stultified plant. But how do we know that is not all right too? A theme is announced. Two basic melodies sound out. One is played through completely with countless variations. Eventually it dies down, not to fade away completely but rather, with the help of the other melody that now rises up, to arise anew in altered dress and reach its fullest expression. The seemingly stunted melody now possesses its full potential for complete development, and it breaks out once again. Is that not a possibility here?

In the history of spirituality and its development, the reform of the Poverello of Assisi undoubtedly is framed within the environment of the famous Gregorian Reform. This reform takes its name from Pope Gregory VII (1073–85), but it actually began some thirty years earlier with the so-called "German popes." Its first great proponent was Leo IX (1049–54), but its greatest impact came with Innocent III (1198–1216) during the lifetime of Francis. One can regard this period of reform as the time when the Church was able to free herself from the overweening power of temporal authority. But such a narrow outlook is in danger of missing the deeper dimensions of the reform movement. At bottom this reform sought to redefine the relationship between the Church and the world in the light of faith. Also involved here was the relationship between faith and rational knowledge, between real-life experience grounded on faith and rational exploration of the data of faith.

In this reform movement we undoubtedly find weighty figures who talked about strict rejection of reason and scholarly science. Such for example was Peter Damian (d. 1072), who was one of the so-called "anti-dialecticians." As I see it, these opponents of scholarship differed from Francis in that they sought to make a new system of their own out of the deposit of faith. This approach was wholly alien to Francis, as we have already seen. He stood simply under the creative activity of God's Spirit, who enabled him to experience the revealed word of Holy Scripture as a message spoken directly to him in the here and now.

Now the question is whether and to what extent a similar process is detectable in the reform of John XXIII. Some may feel it is very rash to set up a parallel between the two reforms. For, the Gregorian Reform spanned a century and its solid results extend down to our own day, while the Johannine reform is scarcely a decade old. Nevertheless it does seem that Vatican II has set in motion a line of development that does not allow for backtracking, even though its end cannot be foreseen.

In this connection one might find some interest in one of the appointments of Pope Paul VI. In May, 1969, the office of secretary of state was given to the sixty-five-year-old French cardinal, Jean Villot, whose doctoral thesis was devoted to the reform of Gregory VII. Recall what happened at Vatican II itself. Somewhat against the desires and interests of the seemingly all-powerful systematic theologians at the Council, the question of the relationship between the Church and the world took over the foreground and ended up with a rousing agreement at the end that swept everything before it. Pointing beyond itself, it promised to be a dynamic force in the future and it has already shown itself to be so. Viewed in this light, the appointment of Cardinal Villot to the chief office in the papal ministry does not seem to be without importance; for he is a man without the customary expertise or inclination for diplomacy. Indeed, if one pictures the Church primarily as a social entity akin to the State, then Villot is the worst possible head-minister imaginable. Only shortly before his appointment, his friend and suffragan bishop was the one and only "worker bishop," Ancel. Villot did not have diplomatic training, nor did he have a diplomatic career; yet these things would seem to be prerequisites for his post. One has only to look at the men who have occupied this post in this century to be convinced of that. Each and every one of them brought along a rich store of experience in the diplomatic field, and they entered this career in their forties at the latest.

It is astonishing that the world at large scarcely took note of the innovative aspect implied in Villot's appointment. Close analysis of a serious nature contradicts the insipid suggestions of the press: that Pope Paul VI, a slow and cautious man given to symbolic gestures, appointed Villot for no particular reason, or out of "francophilia," or in an effort to "internationalize" the curia. One comes closer to the truth in suggesting that this appointment was meant to signalize a changed Church. What the Council had worked out theoretically was now to be fleshed out in a very visible way: i. e., that the primary note of the Church is its spiritual note, not its resemblance to governmental bodies. But this spiritual note does not imply separation from the world; rather, it implies concrete permeation of the world, a work of "service" we would say today.

During the Council itself, Villot was an obtrusive opponent

Picture page 103:
To the birds who were perched motionless on the ground Francis said: "Be grateful to your God, my brothers and sisters! He is your Creator, and you should praise him at all times. He gave you the freedom to fly everywhere. He gave you many and varied forms of dress.... You are indebted to him for assigning the air to you. You do not sow or reap, yet God feeds you. He gives you brooks and springs for drinking, mountains and valleys for shelter, tall trees for nests. And even though you do not stitch or weave, he still clothes you and your fledglings. He must love you very much, since he does so much for you. Take care that you are not ungrateful, my brothers and sisters. Praise God unceasingly."

Sermon to the Birds, fresco by Benozzo Gozzoli (1420–1497), in the apse of the Franciscan church in Montefalco (a national museum today).

Picture pages 104–105:
Having returned from the Holy Land (summer 1220) Francis, weary from his long journey, was riding a donkey. His companion, Brother Leonardo of Assisi, followed behind on foot. He too was tired, and he thought to himself: "My parents and his parents were of the same social class. But he rides while I go on foot and keep an eye on his donkey!" Scarcely had the thought struck him when Francis dismounted and said: "Brother, it is not proper that I ride while you go on foot. You come from a more distinguished house than I do." On the spot Brother Leonardo asked forgiveness from the holy Francis.

Picture page 106:
Francis would often pick up a block of wood and hold it in his left arm as if it were a violin. Using a stick as a bow, he would pretend to play his instrument while he sang French songs in honor of our Lord Jesus Christ. Tears would come into his eyes, and then everything would melt into pure bliss. He would forget what he was holding in his hands and be transported heavenward.

The "holy wood" *(bosco santo)* of Monteluco in the vicinity of Spoleto.

of regal trappings and ceremonies. He moved around the Vatican without any token of his episcopal office, even without his episcopal ring. So alien was this to one Swiss guard that he would not allow this "demythologized" under-secretary of the Council into one general meeting of the secretariat. Now that may seem superficial and unimportant at first glance. But I do not think it is, if one takes the Pope for the man he is. He sees many things which he feels will be realized only step by step over a long period of time. When he can, he is delighted to give expression to them in some broad, all-encompassing symbolic gesture. The appointment of Villot fits in here, in my opinion. It is both a symbolic gesture and a step towards concrete realization.

Today we are so preoccupied with "legal" changes – which we now call "structural changes" – that personal changes on the individual level seem unimportant to us. But what value is there in structural changes, if the new holders of authority are taken from the old structures? What must be changed first is the representatives of authority, then the structures! The most perfect service-oriented structure can turn into a gruesome despotism if it is administered by despots. A service-oriented man can make a despotic structure tolerable, and even change it, because it is intolerable to him even though he appears to be a despot within it.

And so I come to a conciliar theme which is intimately tied up with the Poverello of Assisi. I refer to poverty in the Church, the poor Church, the Church of the poor. Although the three terms do not say the same thing, they were used almost interchangeably by the Council Fathers as if they were synonyms! This topic was on everyone's lips when the Council started. It then retreated into the confines of a small but world-embracing group of bishops and experts, while the vast majority of conciliar participants became embroiled in debates over systematic theology and in questions of church structure. Towards the end of the Council it surfaced once again.

The opposition – or perhaps it would be better to say, the difference – between reform that could be systematized and reform that could not was nowhere more tangible at the Council than on the question of poverty. Even the bishops who were most concerned about this issue did not grasp the difference immediately. They came together in a discussion group which they dubbed the "little ecumene." Others outside this group such as Henri Fesquet, the reporter for *Le Monde,* dubbed it the "catacomb group." Whereas all the other groups divided up more or less along national lines, in accordance with their different interests and languages, basically every continent and land was represented in the "little ecumene." "Ecumene" here had its original Greek sense of "the whole inhabited world."

The predominant bloc of members were representatives of the Third World; the southern half of the globe, the underdeveloped countries. But names well known to us were also participants: Cardinals Liénart and Gerlier (France), Léger (Canada), Lercaro (Bologna), and, before he became Pope, Montini (Milan). The European bishops were led by French-speaking representatives: Ancel, Stourm, Boillot, the future Cardinal Garrone, Hughes, Gujot, Martin, Théas, Gouyon, Gand, and Guerry; also included were the future Cardinal Duval (Algeria), the "Bishop of the Sahara" Mercier, and the Belgian bishop of Tournai, Himmer. The largest number came from South America. They were led by the tireless, charismatic figure of Helder Pessôa Camara, the archbishop of Olinda and Recife and a very close friend of Montini, and by Botero (Medellín, Colombia). It was at Medellín, shortly after Paul VI's visit to Bogotá, that the reform bloc of Latin American bishops won a victory in setting down the future course of the Church there. Africans were present also: e. g., Archbishop Zoa (Yaoundé, Cameroon) and Blomjous (Tanganyika). Representing the eastern rites, practically all the Melchite bishops were present, led by Maximos IV Saigh. India, China, and Japan had at least one or two representatives.

It is worth pointing out that in this little ecumene no great role was played by the question which split the official Council along speculative theological lines and divided people up into progressives and conservatives. The meetings were attended by well-known conservatives, who became zealous champions of the Church of the poor. They included Franic (Yugoslavia), Dwyer (England), Gonzales Martin Marcello (Spain), and Gonzales

Moralejo Rafael (Spain). Then Bishop of Astorga, Gonzales Martin Marcello became the Archbishop of Barcelona in 1967; though not a Catalan himself, he gradually won the heart of the laboring class by his courageous stand against police oppression. Gonzales Moralejo Rafael was then the suffragan bishop of Valencia; since 1967 he has been without a post because of his stance against the regime.

The difference is clear and obvious. In the meetings of the official Council, people dealt with the reform of the system, be it with respect to theology or law. In the meetings of the little ecumene people dealt with the transformation of their life-style and its structure, a transformation that had been or could be felt in charismatic terms. Of course the two streams of thought met when it came down to logical conclusions, agreeing in part and disagreeing in part. The critical area, however, was their differing starting points: theological science or spirituality.

Now that does not mean to suggest that theologians were excluded from the little ecumene. On the contrary, the proponents of poverty besieged the most outstanding conciliar theologians in every discipline. They did so directly on their own, or indirectly through theology students. Among the theologians solicited were: Lyonnet (exegesis), Häring (sociology), Mendizabal (ascetics), Fuchs (moral theology), Mollat (mysticism), Grasso (pastoral theology), Alszéghy (dogmatic theology), Diez Allegria (sociology). Two Dominicans, Congar and Chenu, tried to clarify the theme. The great sociologist of reform, Lebret, worked predominantly for South America. Houtard, the Belgian who later became a friend of Camilo Torres, explored the deeper problems posed by the question and served as an adviser to the bishops.

To be sure, the overall results of all this questioning and research were meager. Many professors explained that they were "not competent" in the subject or that it was still *terra incognita* for researchers. Some said bluntly that it had nothing to do with their speciality. Quite apart from these people, the contributions of those who did look for an answer were unhelpful and unsatisfying for the most part.

Despite this fact, I would like to reproduce a few documents that reveal something of the thinking of these bishops. I fully realize that my presentation is a bit one-sided, but it would take a whole book to record all the statements of these poverty-bishops at the Council. At both the first and second session of the Council there were times when at least one bishop spoke every day about poverty as a reform topic, interjecting it into the discussion in some way with reference to one domain or another: e. g., liturgy, the Church, sanctity, etc. The charismatic cast of these speakers was immediately recognizable. Their words differed markedly from the speeches of others, who always related what they had to say to one scholarly discipline or another. The proponents of poverty usually spoke from their own real-life experience, in a highly unconventional and profoundly concrete way. But what they said could scarcely be compressed into a formula or schema, which the Council would have to arrive at eventually. One could say that the statements and interventions of these bishops were too existential for a conciliar text. Hence they aroused the displeasure of many, for they seemed to impede rather than to promote the forward progress of the Council's labors.

The reader must picture to himself how such a conciliar debate went. Let us take the issue of liturgical reform as an example. Two sides stood over against each other: on the one side, the reformers; on the other side, the immobilists, who were opposed to any and all change. Even the reformers came from liturgical institutes where one knew very exactly all the forms taken by the liturgy in the course of history. They wanted to strip away carefully all the overlays, layer by layer, in order to lay bare its pristine form. Now add the poverty-bishops to this picture. They wanted to get rid of all the pomp that is alien to us and that erects a barrier between priest and people. Everything should speak directly to present-day human beings, and to the poor above all. And that did not mean the poor of a bygone day, who still lived in a patriarchal world and who therefore found their feelings about life embodied and expressed to some extent in regal pomp and in the grandeur of baroque churches and Roman basilicas. No, it meant the poor people of today, who are deeply conscious of the equality of all men, and who think it is only a matter of time before they live as well as the rich do today on every level. The demand to address these people in a living way and on their own level was something unheard of for both the immobilists and the progressive liturgical institutes.

As an example, let me quote an intervention by Juan Iriarte (51), the bishop of Reconquista, Argentina. He spoke at the third session of the Council (24 September 1964) when the reform of the episcopal office was being discussed.

"I bid my brother bishops to 'convert' to the modern world. We are feudal bishops, we must become bishops of the atomic age. The characteristic features of the present-day world are socialization, urbanization, cultural pluralism.... They call, first and foremost, for a new life-style on the part of bishops. The bishop must expend time and effort to become truly acquainted with the world in which he lives.

"To make time for dialogue with his priests, his faithful, and Non-Catholics, he must give up activities of a secondary nature: e. g., consecrating bells. He must learn the idiom of men today. Even the style in which he expresses himself must move towards greater simplicity. His authority must be exercised differently. He must encourage priests and lay people to start a dialogue with him and to undertake initiatives on their own. He must realize that he exercises his authority over grown men, who have a keen sense of their own personal responsibility.

"He must lay particular stress on poverty, not through theatrical gestures, but by introducing a new style into the Church. Today's bishop cannot have anything theatrical about him. He must display the same simplicity as John XXIII."

At this point Bishop Iriarte was suddenly interrupted by the moderator of the session. There was no time for such unseemly attacks! But we know what Iriarte would have gone on to say from an earlier publication of his. An excerpt appeared more than a year earlier in *Le Monde* (1 June 1963):

"'Blessed are the poor.' I regard poverty and the external simplicity of the Church as a prerequisite for the proclamation of her message. The message of the Church always has and always will be conveyed by peace, truth, love, hope, and the spirit of service.

"But then I think: How difficult it is for us bishops of poverty in the Church of Christ to pass on this message today! At the start this message was swaddled in the poverty of Incarnation, crib and cross. It was proclaimed by a working man who had no place to lay his head, who washed the feet of those he called 'friends,' who used the common speech of everyday life when he told the story of the lost drachma.

"Today this message is addressed to people caught in the straitened circumstances of proletarian life. Sixty-five percent of them suffer from hunger. Many of them live in *favelas, barrios bajos,* slums. They are used to calling each other 'comrade' and to hearing the direct, barbed comments of their party leaders. They are used to the sober lines of their skyscrapers and the racy lines of their jet planes. They are used to seeing the 'khakis' of their military commanders when they pass in review.

"And we? We must proclaim this message from the marble precincts of our high altars and episcopal thrones. We must proclaim it amid the baroque proceedings of our pontifical ceremonies, amid the alien ballet of miter and crosier and the even more alien circumlocutions of our ecclesiastical idiom. We parade before our people in purple garb, ride in the newest model cars, occupy first-class apartments. The people address us as 'Your Excellency,' genuflect before us, and kiss the stone in our ring.

"It is not easy to free oneself from this heavy weight of history and tradition. Woe betide the oversimplifiers, who find everything quite simple! Let us be wary of damning others or proposing second-rate solutions. Lord, may we practice meekness, poverty, and simplicity of heart. Through prayer and the protection of your Mother, may we receive from you the full measure of your light and the necessary courage, so that the Church in our day may find its way and flesh out the ideal proposed for it by your servant, John: to be the Church of the poor."

No, such a reform was not envisioned at the Council. For most bishops there was something disturbing and shocking about it, precisely because it posed the reality so concretely. After all, where were the "standards" against which one could measure himself? The poverty-bishops were certainly not mystics in disguise. And many of the proposals put forward in the first months of the Council did have an over-fanciful aspect. One could not expect all the bishops to trade in their valuable crosses for two slivers of wood, to give up all their rings or remove the precious stones in them as the bishops of the Eastern Church did. What value would such signs have? They might indeed eliminate a bit of scandal. But church renewal could only flow from the bedrock of freely chosen acts and a deep inner attitude. Bishop Iriarte himself, regarded as the wild man on this issue by some, had not failed to warn people against the "oversimplifiers." Yet the frightened moderator would not let him finish speaking, so great was he afraid of confronting reality. And the press, it must be said, also omitted the central concluding paragraph of his speech in their report. Even *Le Monde* was guilty of that omission.

The parallel to the initial appearance of the Poverello on the public scene is evident. Then, too, there were cardinals who formed hasty judgments without listening first, publicists who did not go into the matter deeply. "Discernment of spirits" is seldom given to devotees of systematization.

A host of bishops did don a simple wooden cross, or contribute their rings to the cause of the poor. At the end of the Council Pope Paul VI gave a simple, inexpensive ring of unity to all the bishops. This gift undoubtedly represented his unspoken desire to meet the poverty-bishops half-way. Even as pope he continued to bear the stamp of his work in the little ecumene.

In his book, *The Church of the Poor* (1967), Henri Fesquet records such papal gestures and attempts to explain them. He notes Pope Paul's contribution of his personal tiara to the cause of the poor. He also cites various talks of the pope, including one to the bishops of Italy shortly before the end of the Council: "When a bishop, clad with the anachronistic tokens of his office, comes before his people and urges them to follow the gospel, he certainly does not evoke their admiration. Instead they are shocked and scandalized. Let us thank God for everything we have given up in the way of external, temporal goods." And in his first encyclical, *Ecclesiam suam* (6 August 1964), he wrote:

"There are, however, two special points We feel constrained to mention.... The first of them is *the spirit of poverty*.... Zeal for the spirit of poverty is vitally necessary if we are to realize the many failures and mistakes we have made in the past, and learn the principle on which we must now base our way of life and how best to proclaim the religion of Christ. One further reason for Our mentioning it here is the difficulty we all find in practicing it. It is Our intention to issue special canonical regulations on this subject, but We do ask you, Venerable Brethren, for the support of your agreement, your counsel, and your example. It is your task to interpret with authority the movements and inspirations of the Holy Spirit in the Church, and We rely on you to make clear to pastors and people how the spirit of poverty should regulate everything they do and say" (nos. 53–54).

If one agrees with Fesquet's assertion that the Pope was referring solely to two points in this encyclical, poverty and love, then one cannot avoid the conclusion that he was "not quite understood" by the episcopate around the world. In other words, there was no reverberating echo for his words. They were taken as "pious exhortations" that did not call for concrete implementation. Where could he go from there?

The Pope was deprived of advice and concrete example from his colleagues in the episcopate. He did do this and that, to be sure. He took away the outdated armament from his guards and the bizarre red hats from his cardinals. He also curtailed the finery of the latter. The public at large took little notice. What was all that supposed to mean? Was this the right moment to set new fashion-styles, when the structures of the Church were being called into question? Undoubtedly the Pope had a very meaningful goal in mind, but the highly touted collegiality left him in the lurch! Left to himself, he lost courage. In more recent years he gave up talking about the poor Church. And it is no wonder! After all, what is a pope without any echo?

Let us get back to the Council. We live in an age of reflection. However true it may be that the idea of poverty at the Council sprang from intuition, reflection had to enter the picture precisely because of the role of clarity and intelligibility in the present-day world. That step was taken too, though it has not yet reached the end of its journey by a long shot. Here I shall not consider the countless theological efforts devoted to this subject, such as the distinguished contributions that have appeared in *Christus,* a leading Parisian periodical on spirituality (1967). I shall restrict myself to what happened at the Council.

The first thing which deserves mention here is the speech of Cardinal Lercaro (Bologna) near the end of the first session (1962). The Council had finally managed to find its real theme: the Church. Cardinal Suenens had proposed in broad outlines the agenda from which the Council would not swerve in the three years that followed. Then Cardinal Montini had explored the theme more deeply in its theological terms. It was his last speech before he was elected pope. Now Lercaro took the floor. For all his agreement with the theme of the Church, he failed to see in it the line of sight that the little ecumene had sought to give to the Council. Montini indeed had adverted to it, but not as the central concern; for him it was a moral appendage to systematic theological reflections. Something hat to be said now lest the question of poverty become one of those baroque flourishes which were not rare at the Council, and which many regarded as a nod to the past rather than a dynamic force for the future.

Lercaro's speech sent tremors through the Council Fathers, and especially through the press corps. It was like the sudden advent of a spring day, when all the signs of winter point against its arrival. Yet, despite its first impact, this speech was quickly buried under the antique ceremonies that celebrated the close of the first session. It was also buried in the gloomy shadows that gathered around the dying Pope John. Press, radio, and television concentrated on these events and quickly forgot Lercaro's speech. No one found time to translate it or get it into print. So the astonishing and paradoxical thing happened: Lercaro's speech faded out of sight. I have found only one translation of it, and it is rather poor. So I reprint it here in what I hope is a better one:

Venerable Brothers! To begin with, I too should like to em-

phasize and support what Cardinal Suenens and Cardinal Montini have talked about: the aim of this Council, the ordering and delimiting of the topics proposed, and above all the urgency of working out a doctrine on the Church.

We are looking for a teaching on the Church that goes down to bedrock foundations, that goes far beyond the juridical considerations that have shackled the drafts submitted so far.

The result of this session, as I see it, is this. We have spent two months together in open, fraternal, and obliging work of study and research. With the help of the Holy Spirit, this has brought us all to a better understanding of what this Second Vatican Council must present to today's human beings: i.e., the inner mystery of the Church, which is as it were the great *sacrament of Christ, the Word of God, who reveals himself to mankind and who lives, dwells, and works in its midst. I want to direct your attention to the revelation of this mystery of Christ in the Church, this mystery which not only goes on but also takes on historical reality to the highest degree. I would say this: The mystery of Christ in his Church is always, but particularly today,* the mystery of Christ in the poor. *For, as Pope John XXIII has said, the Church is the church of all, but of the poor especially.*

1

As I read through the drafts that were given to us yesterday, I was rather taken aback by an astonishing omission. All the drafts which we have received so far, and which people propose to give us, seem to take no clear account of history and its present thrust in the light of this basic and pristine revelation of the mystery of Christ. But the fact is:

(a) This aspect was presupposed by the prophets to be the authentic sign confirming the mission of the Christ;

(b) It was made public in the birth, childhood, hidden life and public ministry of Jesus;

(c) It represents the foundation and law of the kingdom of God;

(d) It stamps its imprint on any and every outpouring of the Spirit in the life of the Church, from the era of the apostolic

community to times of intensive inner renewal or outer expansion;

(e) It will find its definitive confirmation at the second coming of God's Son in glory, when reward or punishment will be meted out.

So, as we come to the close of this first conciliar session, we must solemnly confess and proclaim this fact: We shall not satisfy our duty or openheartedly respond to God's plan and man's expectations, if we do not focus on the mystery of Christ in the poor and his message and turn it into the central core of our teaching and law-giving, into the very soul of this Council.

2

In terms of the present-day situation this task is concrete, clear, and highly relevant:

(a) By comparison with other ages, today the message of Christ is not proclaimed as zealously to the poor. Their hearts seem to stand over against the mystery of Christ in the Church, more distant and alien.

(b) Yet the mind of man is presently taken up with the mystery of poverty. Driven by dramatic and anxiety-laden questions, he is trying to explore the situation of the poor, be they individuals or nations, who live amid suffering and yet have attained a new awareness of their rights.

(c) Today the poverty of the vast majority (two-thirds of mankind) is flouted by the immeasurable affluence of the minority. The poverty of the masses is despised more and more each day, while sensual men run greedily after more wealth.

Now when I refer to the problem of evangelizing the poor, as others have done before me, I am not trying to add a new topic to an already overladen table of contents in the agenda. I am simply trying to stress two things:

(a) We will not be doing justice to the deepest and most authentic demands of our day, or to our hopes for promoting unity among all Christians, indeed we will be dodging them, if we treat the evangelization of the poor as one conciliar topic among many others!

(b) If the Church is truly the theme of this Council as so many have said, then in full agreement with the eternal truth of the Gospel and our present moment in history we can say: The theme of this Council is indeed the Church, but insofar as she is the "Church of the poor" above all.

3

Having described our subject-matter in this way, I take the liberty of offering the following proposals:

(a) From here on the Council will hopefully devote, not just a part, but the major part of its efforts to working up the gospel's teaching about the holy poverty of Christ in the Church. It should highlight the plan of God, who selected poverty as a sign and a condition. I would maintain that this sign of the presence and saving power of the Word-made-flesh is great in Christ and his Church.

(b) A similar priority will hopefully be given to working out the evangelical doctrine on the special dignity of the poor. They represent privileged members of the Church because the Word of God preferred to conceal his glory in these members until the end of time.

(c) In accordance with the new division of all the doctrinal drafts that many have requested, I hope that in our treatment of every topic the entological entwinement of Christ's presence in the poor with the two other profound realities of the mystery of Christ in his Church will be duly noted and considered. I refer to the presence of Christ in the celebration of the Eucharist, through which the Church is grounded and made one; and to the presence of Christ in the hierarchy, which leads and teaches the Church.

(d) I hope likewise that due notice and consideration will be given to tieups with the context of history in our work on schemata dealing with pastoral methods and the reform of church structures. For, candid and energetic recognition of the special dignity of the poor in God's kingdom and the Church has ever been closely associated with the capacity to evaluate correctly the

potentialities, obstacles, and methods involved in structural reform of the Church.

4

Presupposing all this, I shall conclude by simply citing a few examples of what our reform decrees must effect. They must show prudence and moderation in doing this of course, but they must also do it without compromise or timidity.

(a) Circumscribe the use of material goods, particularly those which in and of themselves tend to obscure holy poverty from sight, in accordance with the axiom: "I have neither gold nor money, but I gladly give you what I do have."

(b) Outline the lineaments of a new life-style or social etiquette for church dignitaries. They must be such that they do not arouse astonished feelings of oddness in people of our time or scandalize the poor. We, who often enough are really poor, should not appear in public as if we were rich.

(c) Foster fidelity to holy poverty in religious orders, both among the individual members and the community as a whole.

(d) Work out a new code of behavior in the realm of economics. We must do away with outmoded institutions of the past that serve no useful purpose and only hinder free, openhearted apostolic effort.

If we prove to be wise and docile with respect to the plan of Divine Providence, if we heed and stress the pre-eminent place of the evangelization of the poor, then it will not be too difficult for us, with the help of the Holy Spirit and the protection of Mary, to find a credible method for presenting the eternal and immutable gospel of God in all its fullness and potency with reference to every problem, be it one of doctrine or practice. In this way it will also be easier for us to gather the whole Christian family into oneness, even as the Father and Son are one. We will speak more deeply to men's hearts; and the hopes of all people today, of the poor in particular, will find fulfillment in the Church of Christ. He, though rich, became poor so that we might be enriched by his grace and glory.

We read Lercaro's words today with a trace of astonishment still. We can understand why even a sober, critical-minded person like Father Rouquette, a French reporter at the Council, could describe it in *Etudes* as "a turning point in the history of the Church." To be sure, the seasoned professor of the history of theology hedged a bit, prefacing his remark with a prudent "perhaps."

And what did come of Cardinal Lercaro's proposed plan? Did the text-revisers utilize the interventions of the poverty-bishops in drawing up the various schemata? No, for the most part they disregarded them completely – simply because they did not readily tie in with the drafts. Did the pertinent commissions, which drew up the drafts, consider their main concern to be work up the gospel doctrine on poverty, to shed light on the ontological tieup between the presence of Christ in the poor, the presence of Christ in the Eucharist, and the presence of Christ in the hierarchy? Did they hold the firm conviction that any and every reform effort in the Church with credible and perduring results has gone hand in hand with respect for the poor, and did they look to that for the criteria that would govern the reform now at hand?

No, they did not pick up these demands posed by Cardinal Lercaro. They were short on time and overworked. In the minds of theologians, such "spiritual" reflections were a borderline-area. Once again, as in the time of Francis of Assisi, *ratio* won out over *contemplatio,* system won out over concrete reality. System won the day at Vatican II.

Lercaro's statement clearly has two parts: a Biblical aspect and a present-day aspect. He maintains that they complement and reinforce one another. The Biblical aspect shows us that according to God's revelation in word and deed the pathway of redemption involves becoming poor, that the poor are the specially favored ones of God, and that the message of salvation must be proclaimed to them above all. The second part says that this is not being done adequately today in the Church, that the Church seems to prefer the rich even though the problem of poverty is racking today's world. Two things follow from this: (1) The

Church itself, as the sign of Christ's redeeming activity, must become poor in an earnest way; (2) The Church must give priority to the evangelization of the poor. That is as far as Lercaro's statement goes.

The problem itself, however, is much broader. Lercaro says nothing about whether the Church should help the poor to be poor no longer. To put it another way: Does the Church have the task of criticizing and changing the existing social structures? The Council firmly committed itself in this direction. One need only read the opening message of the Council Fathers to mankind (1962), and the sections on culture, economics, politics, and societal life in *Gaudium et spes* (1965), to see the hard shell of commitment that encases the Council. It proclaims that the Church must work earnestly for the progress of mankind towards ever greater humanity. And Paul VI, in his closing address to the Council, leaves no doubt that the distinctive mark of Vatican II is its "yes" to the world.

Now one may well ask: How do we reconcile this yea-saying outlook with a "poor Church"? Neither Cardinal Lercaro nor the conciliar texts say anything about this. Texts, embodying one viewpoint or the other, stand alongside each other without any inter-relation. One moment it appears that the Church wants to join in solidarity with the poor, to share their life-style and fate, without considering whether these things could ever be changed. Here "the poor" appear to be a fixed class on this earth, living in a fixed societal framework that goes on unchanged through the centuries. The next moment this viewpoint seems to be traded in for a directly contrary viewpoint. Now the poor are regarded in dynamic terms; poverty is the condition of a portion of mankind, and it must be overcome. The task of the Church is not so much to be a poor Church as to take up the cause of the poor and work for the total elimination of poverty.

There is no doubt that the latter viewpoint corresponds much better with the modern outlook on life. But then it becomes clear that we must start over and reconsider the meaning of all the passages in Holy Scripture which talk about becoming poor as the external manifestation of the God who reveals himself —

starting from the time of the prophets and extending to the coming of the Lord in glory.

It would have been proper for the Council to make a clear, distinctive statement on this matter, but it did not. That may well indicate clearly the relative failure of the poverty-bishops. But one should not think that these questions were not raised in the little ecumene. Realists that they were, these bishops could have swept these questions under the table. They could have pointed out that today two-thirds of mankind suffer from hunger and live in "underdeveloped countries"; that this condition, far from being near elimination, will worsen considerably from now until the year 2000. On the other hand, they could not deny that this seemingly fixed and eternally perduring stratum of society is breaking up more every day. Poverty is disappearing in "developed" countries. A social stratum of propertyless people no longer exists; neither does a stratum of unproductive propertied people exist, to all appearances. And it is they that the gospel is referring to when it talks about the rich.

So here we have a situation where the antithesis between rich and poor has shifted from various social strata within one country to whole nations or continents. Does that mean that the message of the gospel now implies that the Church must shift its center of gravity to the underdeveloped countries? Must these countries be her favorites? Are we obliged to see in them a special presence of Christ? Perhaps. But it is not utopian to envision a day when poverty, as one of the structural elements of human society, will have disappeared for the most part. Where would that leave the Church? How would she then give visible, tangible expression to the *kenosis,* the "self-emptying," of the salvation message? This question was one that could not be bypassed.

Here I shall present two answers that were offered during the period of Vatican II. One was offered by the Dominican, Chenu (Paris), who was greatly concerned about the relationship between the Church and the world. Almost all the well-known Dominicans today were pupils in his school of thought: e. g., Congar, Schillebeeckx, Féret. Chenu is a man of great mind and spirit, but his most important work has been in probing topics from their speculative theological and philosophical side. On 3 April 1963, he wrote the following:

Poverty is certainly an ascesis, but it is not just that. It helps man to remain master over the riches he creates and utilizes. On the traditional scale of values it is a moral mastery which enables us to escape the looming threat of alienation posed by wealth and the perverse tendencies of personal, occupational, and national egotism. In short, it signifies the right use of goods which, according to Aristotle and Marcus Aurelius, is regulated by the virtues of modesty and temperance.

For Christians, poverty is certainly, but not just, a more or less legally specified application of the evangelical counsels, *which is often codified in the rules of a given life-style (e. g., the rule of a religious order). To be sure, we must inscribe it in precepts and legal structures. But Christ is no "moral professor"; he is the prophet of the consummated Messianic age.*

On a higher plane poverty is certainly an imitation of Christ, *but it is not just that. Without doubt the outlook and behavior of Christians has been decisively influenced by the crib of Bethlehem, the workshop of Nazareth, and the vagabond life of the Son of Man who had no place to lay his head. These realities are the pledge of the authenticity of their own way of life.*

Poverty is all these things, to be sure. But if it is to be authentic and effective, it must be underpinned by a hope that leads us to engage ourselves in history, to work for man's freedom and happiness.

This prophetic (today we would say "kerygmatic") outlook explains the gospel complaint against the rich and also indicates its limits. Thus poverty is not primarily an ethical system or institution that could provide us with handy guidelines. Rather, it is the continuing process of the Messianic community calling the world into question, and the world calling the Messianic community into question.

In the great moments of the Church – and today is such a moment – the confrontation becomes terrifying when and if the Church realizes that she is no longer meeting the poor. For they, by definition, are her first charge. Failure to deal with them is not a vexing side-issue. It represents a basic loss, indicating the degeneration of the Messianic community into an established church. What a shock for the Council!

The matter is ticklish. For when poverty calls into question the most legitimate certainties of individuals and institutions, then it is difficult for it to avoid a certain anarchism in which counterfeit spiritualism is clearly intermingled with political ferment. All poverty movements, even those in the Church, are suspect. From the time of St. Francis right down to our own day, dawning awareness of the role of the poor in the Messianic kingdom has continually called forth the oddest conflicts and divisions. Precisely this prototype of any and every poverty, as presented by the Franciscan interpretation of the gospel, cannot be separated from its Messianism – even when it is a question of its exaggerations. As Ricœur has said: "It is impossible to be with the poor without being against poverty." And as one publication of the equipes enseignantes *put it, "poverty becomes manifest only to those who seek to crush it."*

This love for the poor, this Messianic economy, is directed in practice to fight against poverty in building up the world. If there is a criterion here, it is love for the poor in authentic brotherhood. It is only fleshed out through the community on the solid basis of its hope, which defies all alienating riches. For the individual, as for the ecclesial community itself, it is very difficult to bear this witness. It is the witness of Christ himself, who renounced his divine wealth that might have alienated him, in order to become the brother of all men.

In Chenu's words we find that we have plunged deeper in our considerations. Christian poverty is grasped as *eschatological witness.* He points to a dimension which does not show up as a prime motif in Francis' conception of poverty: i. e., poverty as a conscious anticipation of man's final state. Some of his followers, to be sure, had read the writings of Joachim of Fiore (d. 1202) with great enthusiasm. In them this tieup is apparent even though the age of the Holy Spirit, predicted to arrive in 1260, an age in which there would no longer be sacraments or priests but only love, was still not the kingdom of God proclaimed in Holy Scripture. What cannot be denied is that in the time of Francis, and quite independent of him, a dynamic conception of the Church had replaced passive waiting for Christ's second coming among many Christians and even some high prelates. Francis of Assisi clearly lived in the midst of this era. How much contact he may have had with figures like Joachim of Fiore is a moot question. But in any case his life and mission were not grounded on this line of thought.

A second motif in Chenu's view of poverty deserves stress here: i.e., the essentially *social* note of Christian poverty. A person is not poor for his own sake; a person loves poverty because he loves all men. Only by establishing solidarity with the poor can he give expression to this. Here, according to Chenu, is the authentic core of Christ's poverty. It is expressed both in the theological *kenosis* of God (emptying himself in the Incarnation and taking on the "form of a servant") and in the earthly life of Jesus (preaching the gospel to the poor and eating with publicans and sinners). Hence, the obligation of the Church to be a poor Church. Here we see clear points of contact with the saint of Assisi.

Finally we see a third motif in Chenu's presentation that scarcely entered the mind of the Poverello: establishing *solidarity with the poor* in order to conquer poverty here and build up the world. That does not mean this brand of poverty is false or unchristian. On the contrary, it can signify a thoroughly legitimate and indeed necessary extension of Franciscan poverty.

The second response to the problematic issue of poverty came from Cardinal Lercaro once again. He gave it in a speech at the third session of the Council (4 November 1964), when the Council Fathers were debating the stance of the Church vis-a-vis culture.

Paragraph 22 of our draft (the first and best draft of the Pastoral Constitution on the Church and the World, the second draft of which appeared only in the last session in 1965) is more or less a model for the whole text. For, it touches upon a most important question which synthesizes and makes clear that the

Church and the world are distinct from one another and yet closely intertwined.

In other words, a very profound and difficult problem shines through at every point: Why and in what sense is divine revelation needed for progress in human knowledge, so that man's knowledge... may become ever more human? On the other side of the coin: Why and in what sense does human progress, even in the realm of secular knowledge, contribute to the analogous clarification and development of revealed truth?

The studious efforts of the commission in working up the draft deserve praise. Yet the text is not wholly satisfactory. It stops precisely where it should begin.

We read in this text that culture is of the highest importance to the Church today, that the Church derives great benefits from culture. For that reason the Church looks upon scientific, technological, and artistic progress with an unprejudiced and confident eye. That is not enough! Nor is it enough to add that the Church is very interested in seeing that cultural progress develops "correctly," that harmonious balance between different cultures is preserved, and that progress does not run counter to "integral humanism" (Maritain) or an appropriate cultural pluralism. [Pope Paul VI discusses these aspects in his subsequent encyclical, Populorum progressio.] All these statements are platitudes. They do not say very much and they are not adequate to provide for an authentic encounter between the Church and culture. And when I say "culture," I do not mean the culture of a bygone age. I mean the culture of today and tomorrow. For this to be a genuine encounter that will perdure and grow, we must first of all analyze and evaluate certain changes in the whole educational system — something in which the Church is vitally concerned. Such changes are obviously a basic prerequisite for the present-day situation of culture.

1

First and foremost, the Church must acknowledge that in the realm of culture she is poor and strives for ever greater poverty.

Here I am not talking about material poverty, but about a

logical consequence of evangelical poverty in the realm of ecclesial education. As is the case in giving up certain customs and inherited values, here too the Church anxiously preserves certain treasures of a bygone age. These treasures are glorious things, of course, but they are no longer quite in keeping with the mental outlook of the present age. Examples are scholastic, philosophical, and theological systems; pedagogical and academic principles; study curricula that are still in use at ecclesiastical universities; methods of research; and so forth. If necessary, the Church must have the confidence to renounce these "treasures" or devaluate their importance, to avoid boasting of them and rely on them only sparingly. For, these treasures often hide the light of the gospel message under a haystack instead of displaying it on a lampstand. They often pose obstacles to the expansion of the Church that could come from the achievements of a new culture or the treasures of older cultures that have blossomed outside the borders of Christendom. Those ancient treasures can restrict the universality of the Church's dialogue, can divide more than unite, can exclude human beings rather than attract and convince them.

I certainly am not asking for an impoverished theology, or for a poverty of mere nay-saying. The distinction between evangelical poverty and subhuman poverty holds true in the realm of cultural education too. I yearn, not for subhuman poverty, but for evangelical poverty; not for ignorance and narrow-mindedness, but for sobriety and singlemindedness. I yearn for nimbleness of spirit, for breadth of mind, and for the daring to set out on new pathways with all the risks entailed. I yearn for purity of mind and modesty, which go to make up the truest and richest spiritual wisdom, as well as authentic historical realism and the keenest feel for concrete reality.

Finally, I do not seek a renunciation of our cultural heritage for the sake of renunciation itself. I seek a renunciation which will win us new treasures and, judged by purely human standards, greater keenness of intellect and preciseness.

The Church has always maintained that it does not identify itself or its teaching with one system, with a particular philosophy or theology. Up to the present, however, the resultant distinction has been recognized more de jure than de facto.

Now it is time to do this in fact; to make clearer the separation of the Church and its essential message from a specific cultural "organon" which many men of the Church, out of a spirit of possessiveness and self-satisfaction, still seriously maintain to be immutable and universally valid.

In order to open up to an authentic dialogue with present-day culture, the Church, in the spirit of evangelical poverty, must make its education more and more flexible. It must turn more and more to the supernatural treasures of Holy Scripture and of Biblical ways of thinking and speaking. The Church must not entertain the fear that she will be less understood for doing this, or that she will disappoint people. If we look at the matter clearly, they really expect nothing else from the Church. In this way the culture of the Church will eventually cease to look like rationalism or some reliance on scholarly science of secular provenience. Instead it will represent a highly effective religious force that is capable of leavening any present or future culture.

2

From what I have said so far, it is immediately evident that ecclesial education must strike out on a new course. We must introduce a new paideia into the Church, above all into its own training institutions (seminaries, novitiates, etc.), and into scholarly research.

Now that relates to the very core of our draft. How can we hope for a continuing and future-oriented dialogue if the spokesmen of the Church, be they priests or lay people, continue to be educated by a study curriculum that is wholly out of touch with reality? If the scholarly idiom in which they are supposed to think, for all its venerable age, is dead and buried, is no longer a universal idiom capable of expressing the modern idiom that dominates the whole world today?

From the very core of this schema, from the themes that it sets forth, it follows that reforms are necessary. Without such reforms no one will believe that we are serious about this topic {dialogue *with the world!}. Without such reforms no one will believe that we really welcome the authentic achievements of culture.*

3

The themes of this age once again! They require that we revive an old tradition in the Church, the tradition of bishops who were both shepherds and theologians (doctores) *at the same time. This must gradually become the commonplace thing once again. For centuries Christian culture was for the most part the work and product of great bishops, who stood out by virtue of the fact that they were simultaneously great pastors and great teachers. Even when we take into account the important institutions of the waning medieval age and the modern age, the fact remains that the purest and most authentic form of ecclesial education did not come from them alone. It came at least as much from the teaching rostrum of bishops who were "theologians." And here I mean "theologians" in the most authentic and pristine sense of the term. I am not referring to those who can only speak about God in scholastic terms. In short, we must get back to the full and complete image of the bishop (at least insofar as that depends on us and not directly on God, especially with regard to the selection of bishops). We must get back to the image of bishops who are men of the spirit; men suffused with pneuma ("spirit") who converse with God and who fashion the essential tenets of their leadership and teaching office out of this interior experience; men truly capable of interpreting and explaining the condition and the import of an age, a people, a culture....*

In a fourth section Cardinal Lercaro again refers to the collaborative work of lay people in the realm of theology. He insists that the Church must dedicate time and effort to the training of lay theologians, and that these lay theologians must be given teaching positions in the graduate faculties of theology. Theology should not remain a monopoly run by the clergy. Lercaro also insists that the Church establish theological institutions wholly run by the laity, with the hierarchy supervising of course. To these institutions the clergy would be sent for training.

This speech by Lercaro points up another side of Christian

poverty. He relates it only to the realm of culture, but it can be applied to other areas quite readily: e. g., church structures. The core of his thought is clearly that poverty ultimately comes down to what is very much a *spiritual outlook and attitude.* It means that the Church as the bearer of Christ's message, for all her "incarnation," cannot and may not ever identify herself with a specific form of culture that is tied to a certain time or place. The Church participates in every form of culture. She cannot help but express herself in one of the languages that is on hand. And here language does not mean simply words, sentences, and stylistic devices. Dress, bearing, life-style, music, painting, architecture, and many other things are also language. That is, they are the communication and expression of the individual person and a whole people. All these things are not the Church, but the Church must be in all of them. Her poverty resides in the fact that in these areas she has nothing of her own to point to besides these languages, that she must proclaim her message in all these languages. To be sure, this message signifies the fulfillment of all these languages and bespeaks their limitations. It calls them all into question precisely because it is given expression in other languages as well. Thus it offers criticism of them all, even though it is also the bond that unites them all.

The Church herself is called into question the moment she shows herself incapable of expressing her message (i. e., herself, for what else is she but a message) in one or another human language. Then there is some question whether she has remained loyal to her essential poverty. Is it possible that she tied herself so tightly to a specific culture (e. g., medieval scholasticism, baroque forms, feudal social structures, a mythologized world view, the pre-industrial age), that she has confused her message with this language and now clings fiercely to cultural treasures that hide her light instead of displaying it?

It is astonishing to note how closely Cardinal Lercaro and Father Chenu agree in their statements. To be sure, Lercaro's conception calls for extraordinary clear-headedness on the part of Christians, of bishops in particular as he underlines. They must be men suffused with *pneuma,* men who enjoy and use the God-given gift of the Spirit. Led by the Spirit, the Christian becomes aware of his divine sonship (Rom. 8,14), calls God his father (Gal. 4,6), and gains access to Him (Gal. 1,18). *Pneuma* is intimately bound up with prophecy, with an interpretation of contemporary events derived from concrete experience of God. In this sense *pneuma* is a dynamic thing, an eschatological gift that is already present as "pledge" and "firstfruits."

Now it is precisely here that the poverty-bishops of Vatican II (whose spokesman was Cardinal Lercaro), Father Chenu the Dominican, and Francis of Assisi meet. Grounded on God's *pneuma,* Francis became the prophet of his age. He clearly put inner experience of God higher than the legalistic structures of other Orders, which people tried to impose on him again and again; higher than the thinking of systematic theology which labored to explain God's revelation by mere reason; higher than a world at war over wealth and gold, which tend to foster aggression. In this respect he was the poorest of the poor, and the radicalness of his poverty had no equal.

Nevertheless he did not give way to fanaticism or excessive spiritualism. And this is important to note, for Chenu is right when he points out that soul-felt recognition of the role of the poor in the Messianic kingdom almost inevitably gives rise to tendencies that are a mixture of false spiritualism and political activism and that fall prey to anarchism.

The parallel to events in our own day is clear to see. I do not say this to pass judgment on student disorders, sit-ins in churches, seminary rebellions, or Camilo Torres and his friends. They may well have gone beyond proper bounds, but that does not concern us here. I bring the matter up here for precisely the opposite reason. I want to point out that a real poverty-movement underlies these currents, and that it is a Christian movement in the last analysis. They all seek to give up the present level of achieved ownership because it hinders recognition of human dignity, because it "manipulates" human beings, because it represses man's further development.

No one should dispute the fact that this underlying feeling

pervades all the present-day signs of unrest. They can be considered Christian to the extent that they give concrete form to a hope which, wittingly or unwittingly, points to an eschatological goal; in short, to the extent that they evince awareness of a vocation calling mankind to overcome the flawed situation in which it finds itself. Such an awareness includes within it the hopeful expectation that man will manage to go above and beyond himself. And this hopeful expectation, despite the fact that it truly does reside within man innately, can only find its basis in an unmerited promise from the Absolute. To this Absolute we give the name "God," who reveals himself to us. We affirm him when we, out of hope, equate ourselves with the poor. When I surrender my self and my whole person to such a hope then, in Christian terms, I make an act of faith. Or, to put it another way: In concretely coming to know the poor we come to experience God.

It is the experience of Francis himself. On his trip to Rome Francis traded clothes with a beggar and tried out his way of life for a day in front of a church. In a fit of rage over the stinginess of the rich, he threw all the money he had with him to the poor, and felt happy with his new group of companions. When he did these things, he concretely experienced God and God's desire to make men rich, his absolute promise to carry man above and beyond himself, his eschatological promise. One could say that it was a concrete, personal *experience* of eschatology, of the wealthy God who chooses to share his wealth. Later, when Francis shrank from kissing the hand of a leper and helping him, he heard God whispering to him within: "I will teach you that the bitter is sweet." But in what lay the sweetness and the bliss? Certainly not in being poor as such, or in kissing a leper! It lay in the confident hope that poverty and leprosy are overcome in the kingdom of God, that is, in faith in God's absolute promise to man. And the appropriate response on man's part is absolute self-surrender, which found expression in Francis as complete poverty and unreserved assistance to the poor man and the leper. It is only with this self-renunciation that the promise is truly and fully *experienced*.

It is obvious enough that fanaticism lies close at hand for people who surrender themselves to such an experience. Poverty movements arise in which the meaning of the whole is obscured. Poverty is sought for its own sake, for some such motive as contempt for material things. Any and all effort to improve man's lot is rejected. The devotees bid goodbye to all scholarship, order, organization, structure, authority, and culture. Failing to grasp its authentic meaning, one falls prey to anarchy or to some utopia.

Some might claim that the present day is not threatened very much by this kind of poverty movement. For, the whole thrust of the revolutionary movement today is clearly aimed at improving man's lot and recognizing his personal dignity and freedom. People feel frustrated and would like to remove the causes of this frustration. But even here there lurks a possible misunderstanding of the true sense of poverty. People believe they can bring about a society without authority or structure. They seek to release man from any and all restrictions. This is not simply a reaction to an overly structured society produced by our technological age. Underlying it also is the fact that a shift in human awareness has taken place. People now tend to say that man has "come of age." This is also connected with the worldwide spread of information agencies. It is a product of the technology and organization that now holds sway in the world.

Thus the revolution of our day is not simply a revolution against technology, even though it is directed against a use of technology that seems to manipulate man and run counter to his new-found "mature" awareness. We could say that the progress of science and scholarship has altered man's consciousness in a fundamental way, due to their practical applications. This in turn calls for a transformation of human structures. As Vatican II put it: "We are witnessing a new humanism, in which man is characterized by personal responsibility for his fellow men and history." And the awareness of a new personal responsibility calls for new rights. One of our favorite expressions is that every right also signifies a responsibility. But the opposite is also true: Every responsibility implies a new right.

So far so good. But what are the limits of this development? What is the measuring rod? How do we avoid anarchy and utopia? Today we find more than a few people talking about the necessity of utopias. I have met starry-eyed young people who proclaim quite openly that they are utopians. As they see it: "Only utopia moves the world forward." That is the modern version of false spiritualism! Indeed it is a sober and carefully calculated version, because these people know very well that neither they nor later generations can achieve what they claim to be striving for. What they mean is that only utopia is capable of unmasking the flaws of the present-day world. But precisely that seems impossible to me, for utopian dreams do not unveil anything.

I could agree with them only if I insert here a distinction that is proper to Christians. This distinction points out that the final stage of the kingdom of God can never be fashioned by man, that it is therefore utopian in terms of all man's efforts and the dynamic of history. At the same time, however, this utopia does truly become a reality in the end, not as a product of man's efforts but as a gift promised by God. But if that is true, why should I expend effort in trying to make it a reality? I can wait for a promised gift, but I cannot work for it. That was the attitude of good Christians for a long time. As upright men they did work in the world, but they were not seriously interested in its improvement. Vatican II rejected this attitude, but there are no direct words to justify this.

On the other hand, we may be able to offer an indirect justification. For, God's promise does not have to do with something that is wholly different from human development and unconnected with it. However much it may lie above and beyond man's power, it also lies in the dynamic line along which this power unfolds and develops. So even though it cannot be achieved by these powers, it is in fact their secret standard or goal. But there is even more here! The *gift* which this promise signifies is given to a being with mind and spirit; it is not just planted there. This being must know how to value the gift and be able to comprehend that it represents his fulfillment. But he can and will do this only to the extent that he has expended effort to attain this gift and has suffered from not possessing it. That is why the kingdom of God does not really interest many people; because they have not come to realize that it represents the fulfillment of their efforts in the best sense of that word. That is also why the Christian must necessarily commit his enthusiasm and effort to humanizing the world, and why he must suffer deeply from any and all forms of inhumaneness.

It was certainly a great mistake that for so long Christians worked with the model of a completely dispassionate man who had "overcome himself," who could no longer weep with those who mourned nor rejoice with those who were rejoicing. This withered and moribund man is a bad risk for receiving the kingdom of God. I do not know whether he can really be a part of it at all.

Have I strayed from my theme? Not at all. For the poor are precisely those who hunger and thirst after justice, who put all their energy and passion into improving the lot of man and working for ever greater justice.

May we not assume that the closer humanity gets to its goal, the faster will be the pace of development? Just as the velocity of a falling stone increases as it gets closer to the ground. May we not establish a connection between this principle and the dizzying acceleration of man's development over the last one hundred and fifty years?

Of course, man's goal is already operative in our midst, even though I called it a gift. It works powerfully on us, drawing us on and dwelling within us. Since the time of Jesus Christ, the kingdom of God is already present. The message of Jesus offers nothing but that assurance: The kingdom of God is at hand! It is not present in its fullness or perfection, it is not plain to be seen, but it is present and growing. Vatican II never wearied of citing Paul's remark to the Ephesians about this. No less than sixteen times it reminds us that we are working, "until we all attain... to mature manhood, to the measure of the stature of the fulness of Christ" (Eph. 4,13).

By that the Council understands the development of not only

the individual but also the community of the Church in history. It concerns the coming to maturity of the individual within the community, as Paul's next verse clearly indicates. But God's grace is not operative solely in the Church; it is operative in all human beings, and all have a share in God's kingdom. So when we talk about modern man "coming of age," can we not see this as a stage in the coming of God's kingdom, as a moment in salvation history? The "already present" aspect is being experienced more intensely than ever before in the collective consciousness of mankind, and on a worldwide scale. But so is the "not yet present" aspect, by which I mean the vast store of injustice and poverty that is still around!

The present moment in history is quite comparable to the time around 1200 when Francis was alive. Today as then, world history is taking another step forward towards maturity. That earlier step embraced the world of Christianity in the West. The step today embraces the whole world. That earlier step, as Chesterton suggested, released the world from the daimonic hold of paganism. The step today is releasing the world from social bondage. In that earlier movement the over-enthusiastic dreamt of the "kingdom of the Holy Spirit"; in the movement today utopian dreamers talk about the classless society and the soviet republic. In both cases the visionaries are too hasty and unrealistic in anticipating the end result; but in both cases they are on the right track. The kingdom of God fills men's hearts: the visionary men of our day, the spiritualists of that earlier day, all the poverty movements of that age. It does in fact draw tangibly near and closer to our experience. And one is not off the track in attributing a more mature outlook to our contemporaries than to the men of the thirteenth century, even though the latter spoke explicitly of God while the former regard him as absent or dead.

I think that such a view of history has its justification, even though it is overlooked by all the alien overgrowths that distort it until it is no longer recognizable, even though we miss it at first glance because it looks like a picture-puzzle. But once this basic thrust is recognized, then many things fall into place by themselves. In many of the things that bewilder and frighten us

Picture page 139:
In the "Canticle of Brother Sun" Francis makes special note of the variegated colors of the flowers when he is praising Sister Earth. Celano relates that when Francis found groups of flowers clustered together, he gave them pious exhortations as if they could understand him. Celano goes on the say: "In some wondrous way not given to others, he found entry into the secret mystery of things. To him was given the glorious 'freedom of the sons of God.'" When he saw a flower by itself, he thought of the "shoot from the stump of Jesse" (Is 11,1); and he wanted the friar who was tending the garden to maintain a flower-bed at all times. As Francis saw it, every creature cries out to us and tells us that God made it for us human beings; but this was especially true of flowers.

Picture page 140:
Francis could also furnish his friars with names taken from plants. One praiseworthy name of this sort was Brother Juniper, whom Francis esteemed highly for his selfless kindness that swept all before it: "I wish we had a whole forest of 'Junipers' in our ranks." But he also had unpleasant names for some. There was lazy Brother Drone, noisome Brother Fly, and obstinate Brother Thistle (see picture). He called Brother Leo "little lamb of God" on account of his gentleness; but he also called him "Leo" (lion) to balance off the picture.

we suddenly recognize God's puzzling and tortuous ways. Here and there his countenance seems to have been pulled tight into a grimace, but it is his way and his countenance after all. It does not seem as gruesome as it appeared at first glance. This is important and fundamental if one now proposes to say concretely what should take place today.

We have already put forward a few of the elements. *In negative terms:* Operating out of complete inner freedom and drawn on by the final stage of God's kingdom, we must calmly let go of all those things that gave stability to earlier days but now hinder us from moving closer to a worldwide setup that is more in accord with human dignity. This act would be akin to that of the young Francesco, who dropped his clothes at his father's feet and went out to face a new life: "Now God alone will be my father." *In positive terms:* We must now implement any and every measure that will enable us to promote greater human dignity for all men. Such, for example, would be a new code of law for international trade; or a new labor law designed to take into account the differences existing between different continents, nations, and work situations, such as that which the International Labor Organization (ILA) sought to work out in June 1969. In his encyclical *Populorum progressio,* Pope Paul VI concerned himself with this very program. One can glean specific guidelines from that encyclical. Here I shall quote one section that summarizes the issue:

"What are less than human conditions? The material poverty of those who lack the bare necessities of life, and the moral poverty of those who are crushed under the weight of their own self-love; *oppressive political structures* resulting from the abuse of ownership, of the improper exercise of power, from the exploitation of the worker or unjust transactions.

What are truly human conditions? The rise from poverty to the acquisition of life's necessities; the elimination of social ills; broadening the horizons of knowledge; acquiring refinement and culture. From there one can go on to acquire a growing awareness of other people's dignity, a taste for the spirit of poverty, an active interest in the common good, and a desire for peace. Then man can acknowledge the highest values and God himself, their author and end. Finally and above all, there is faith – God's gift to men of good will – and our loving unity in Christ, who calls all men to share God's life as sons of the living God, the Father of all men" (no. 21).

Now it seems to me, and it is also intimated by these words of Pope Paul VI, that the primary and fundamental thing right now is to fashion a *new awareness*. Criticism of the Vietnam war and of the treatment of underdeveloped countries, together with the hostile reaction such criticism has evoked, clearly point up the fact that a sense of personal responsibility for any and every violation of human rights anywhere in the world has not yet become a worldwide reality. On the whole we are not aware of the tasks and responsibilities confronting us. When Vatican II proclaimed a dawning change in human awareness, it was anticipating matters a bit. Its vision left out of account the contradictory pieces of evidence.

It is quite evident that the Church herself must submit to this contemporary process of change and upheaval. Much is being said and written today about structural changes in the Church, its fuller democratization, an altered conception of authority, the greater maturity of the laity, and the changed status of the clergy. All these things not only can but must be ranged under the thrust of the poverty-movement that is evident today.

One can of course maintain that there is an important – some would say, critical – difference between our own day and the medieval period. In those days the movement for reform welled up from a general awareness that was hardly reflected upon; today it is based upon the precise analyses of sociologists and political scientists. No one can overlook them with impunity. All, including Christians, are obliged to take their investigations into account. Take the conflict in Vietnam, for example. How could the Church manage to know for which side she should take a stand without painstakingly precise analysis of the historical, economic, sociological, political, cultural, and psychological factors at work in Vietnam itself, the Soviet Union, the United States, and China? But the same thing holds true on a smaller scale too, even when it is a question of what concrete measures can be implemented effectively in a relatively small and homogeneous diocese or parish.

The exact sciences have wrested power from the mystics. Where is there room for a figure like the Poverello of Assisi? It is a pleasant memory, perhaps evoking homesickness but certainly not pointing us towards the future.

I know that many people feel this today. They divide people into realists and visionary, charismatic utopians. The most they will concede is that both do have a function in the Church and our society. But it is the analytic realists who must take the lead in deciding what we should do. The charismatic figures are to inject some warmth into their cold logic, nourishing our hopes and quickening our forward progress. That much is granted to them condescendingly.

In reality, however, the division of labor is wholly different. What I hope for is realistic charismatics. And I use the term advisedly. I mean realistic charismatics, not charismatic realists. To be sure, we do need all the scholarly analysts and hardnosed critics. It is shameful and inexcusable that this basic feature of our day is shown little and often no respect from the Church. We have words of praise for the scientist and the scholar. We assure them that there can be no contradiction between faith and scholarship, because all truth comes from God who is their unifying source. And with this encomium uttered, we go about our business as if these highly praised disciplines did not exist at all. No account is taken of them when we set out to restructure the Church, to reform the liturgy, or to educate our children. Our theoretical principle is fundamentally right; our practical activity is sheer madness. That is the source of most of the complaints which maintain that the Church is untruthful and unworthy of belief. Untruthful she is not, unworthy of belief she may well be.

Today the Church must take seriously the data of the scholarly sciences, the analyses of social and political matters, and the achievements of technology. First, so that she will know where to step in with her message. Secondly, so that she will know how to deal with these achievements and what can or cannot be accomplished with their help.

Let me cite, as an example of what I am talking about, the conciliar decree on the media of social communication (*Inter mirifica*). Our hearts are moved when we read there that the Church wants and is obligated to use these outstanding instruments for the propagation of the truth. But these instruments are not suitable for the propagation of every truth. Moreover, careful consideration must be given to the reactions of a pluralistic society, because the mass media do not exist in a sacral realm where a captive audience is addressed. These matters and other similar issues, which presuppose exact knowledge of the instruments of communication, are not mentioned at all in *Inter mirifica*. The fact is that the knowledge is simply not there.

All these facts are true, and we cannot stress enough how different our age is from that of Francis in this respect. Yet, for all that, the kernel of any renewal in the Church cannot be sought there because it must be a Christian renewal after all. What the Christian element is, however, cannot be taken from a handbook of dogmatic or moral theology either. These handbooks, which propose to present a Christian or Catholic system that remains ever the same, do have their own merits. But they also show how much has changed, depending on the age and surrounding circumstances. One issue comes sharply to the foreground at this point, only to withdraw into the background later. One tenet takes a vigorous upswing, another fades out.

At any rate the fact is that the development of the deposit of revelation in the consciousness of the Church has not been a straight-line development. It has always shown a dependence on the conceptual models and structures of the world. Only with difficulty did divine revelation manage to stand out in relief against this backdrop, and it never managed to do so with clarity. Errors and tragic mistakes followed in its wake, but they were presented as logical conclusions deriving from revelation itself.

But where was the criterion of authentic developments? What is the criterion for developments that burrow deeper into revelation and bring up perduring treasures? What is the criterion for developments that find a form – be it in words, structures, or methods – that happily fits a given age and then falls away, as it should, because it threatens to become more of a hindrance than a help? Basically we have only one such criterion: the activity of the Holy Spirit. At least that is the only criterion given to us in Holy Scripture.

We prescind from this fact when we maintain that no proposition contradicting revelation can be believed as revelation by the whole Church. The predication of this "negative" assistance from the Holy Spirit is an attempt to demarcate some sort of legal borderlines for the Spirit. But such an approach can never make clear the *midpoint* of God's activity. It must be something positive, which cannot be circumscribed so easily. For Christian truth is not a system or an ideology. Our "salvation" is not a logical conclusion flowing deductively from a system; rather, it is a gift offered anew to us over and over again. It is the Spirit of God, who was promised to us by the Lord and who "ushers us" into that which an earlier age could not grasp.

Nothing could be more wrong-headed than to picture the Holy Spirit as a kind of "chief ideologist" in the Church, who speaks to us through the pope. The Holy Spirit is more of an "anti-ideologist," in that he repeatedly breaks out of all the Church's ideologies – often in an unexpected fashion. That is precisely the kind of activity that Lercaro was talking about when he spoke about our need for a new type of bishop. Ideologies, too, belong to those "treasures" that the Church must renounce. Again and again she will erect systems; again and again she will be tempted to present her system as a datum of revelation.

Today people say that there are in fact only two ideologies left: the Christian ideology and the Communist ideology. But it is already dawning on us that the Church's Christian ideology will be snatched away from her as she moves into the future, even as the young man's linen garment was snatched away from him on Mount Olivet. Like him, the Church will have to flee naked. Understandably enough, this prospect terrifies more than a few people. But it can be a dispensation of the Holy Spirit for all that. The linen garment of ideology in which the Church is wrapped is not her life. When her "hour" comes, she will have to divest herself of her ideology. That, too, is part of her *kenosis* and her poverty.

But to return to my question: What is the criterion of authentic renewal? Cardinal Lercaro tells us that we need men of the Spirit, pneumatic men, who speak with God and fashion the authentic intuitions of renewal out of this inner experience. I cannot escape the conclusion that this speaking with God, and the experience it entails, represents the authentic core of every genuine renewal and every genuine poverty-movement.

Now this fact may well lead a man of the spirit like Henri de Lubac to refuse to give any answer when he is asked: What will the saint of the future look like? In a book on the mystery of Christian life (1967) he writes: "That is something that entirely escapes our natural foresight and even prophetic intuition." Appealing to the activity of the Holy Spirit, he cites these words of Bernanos: "Holiness is the work of the Holy Spirit, who is not the pale, hazy, timeless sun of enlightened reason offering retrospect or prognosis. He ever remains the Spirit who blows where he will, when he will, and how he will. He is innovativeness itself, the eternal and incomprehensible newness of God."

That is certainly correct. But does that mean we cannot presuppose or intimate anything in advance? Does the "freedom" and "newness" of the Spirit's activity reside in the simple fact that it contradicts reason? I simply cannot believe that. After all, what did Pope John XXIII mean by "signs of the time"? What did the Council mean by "signs of the present day"? There are such signs. Granted that we need a *sensus fidei,* the eye of faith, to see them. But the person who does perceive them can have a presentiment about the pattern of tomorrow's saint, at least in its broad outlines.

One need only recall the age of St. Francis. Before Pope Innocent III met him, he had already glimpsed the activity of the Holy Spirit, the design of God, in the many and varied poverty-movements of the day – even though many human and even heretical ingredients were intermingled in them, along with political motives and changing cultural factors. Innocent III was

Picture page 149:
At the window of the eleventh-century cathedral in Assisi a dog takes the sun lazily and looks out on the Piazza Bevagna below. One will never get to understand Umbria and its people unless one takes due note of the imperturbability of the Italians as well as of their impulsiveness. A dog in church does not disturb them any more than a mother feeding a baby at the breast. What takes first place always is the reality of life as a whole, which cannot be divided up into neat, rational compartments. For all the harshness of his self-surrender to a God who surpasses all limits, Francis always remained truly human and never put excessive demands on anyone.

Picture page 150:
"Wherever we go, Brothers, we always have our cell with us. The body is our element; and our soul is the secluded den that stays in its element in order to pray to God and think about him."
Francis of Assisi

Friar in contemplation in the cloister of the hermitage at Greccio.

no saint, but he was a man of faith. He tried to dig out the sound core of this movement, but could not. Yet this preparatory work helped him to see and acknowledge Francis as the holy man he had been waiting for.

Now it seems to me that the eye of faith today can anticipate the saint of the future too. But it must truly be the eye of faith, not mere speculation. To that extent Henri de Lubac is right when he reacts vigorously against the manipulation of public opinion in such a way that one cannot tell whether talk about the poor Church of the future stems from deep faith or from mere delight in criticism and the instinct for anarchism. Distinguishing the two is not an easy task, particularly since the two may well be intermingled with each other.

At this point many will appeal to the Church's *magisterium*, and there is nothing wrong in that. Yet here again we must be careful to avoid overhastiness. In other words, it is not enough to rest content with accepting and carrying out what the magisterium and the hierarchy command or advise. That would not be Catholic. Consider again the example of Francis of Assisi. It is true that he never said or chose to do anything that ran counter to the authorities of the Church. In all humility he sought their approval, even when he was not strictly obliged by law to do so. To that extent one is quite correct in saying that any interpretation of Francis as a Protestant before his time does not correspond to the historical facts. But he did not live out his evangelical life-style because church authority had recommended or commanded it! He lived it because he had come to experience the gospel concretely in this way and no other. He was a man who had been directly encountered by God's word, and he went on to develop and live his life from there.

It is most important to pay close attention to this fact. Church authority evinced a wait-and-see attitude, and it often leaned towards refusal. That did not stop Francis at all. To a certain extent church authority functioned as a *norma negativa* for him. There was no question of his going against its teaching or instructions. Indeed he issued fearful prescriptions against friars who stubbornly turned their attention to heretical viewpoints. Francis was securely sheltered in the bosom of church authority. But its function for him was to protect and sanction him; the impetus to set out on his way did not come from it. That he got directly from his concrete experience of God.

Now that, I believe, is a pristine Catholic approach. Thanks to the Holy Spirit, there are different gifts from God called charisms. Each of them in its own way helps to build up the people of God. In practice at least, we have lost our awareness of the necessity of these different gifts in the Catholic Church. To be sure, we will admit that these "extraordinary" vocations do crop up "here and there." And we rest content with that because we, after all, are not extraordinary. The one and only charism that remains is church authority. So we load all the rest onto it, and it is often quite willing to take all the gifts that we, not God, offer it. For us this approach is a security blanket; for church authority it is a temptation to unlimited self-assertiveness. Today people are disputing the authority of church authorities. But in fact they may only be concerned about those other gifts of God which the Church needs just as much, but which church authority has illegitimately arrogated to itself. It will not readily give up these hoarded treasures; it will only be able to do so if these charisms develop once again from below.

Every human being has a share in some such charism, in some experienced vocation to service within the community, which he must answer for before God and which entails more than simply hearing and following the instructions of the Church. That is what gives rise to the people of God which Vatican II talked about. The attitude of poverty which everyone must evince in doing this consists in giving up the security we are accustomed to feel in relation to our good behavior. We must give up this narrow-minded, self-centered security in favor of an inner, experimental encounter with God, who bids us to dare one thing or another through self-surrender to others. We tremble when we hear the call. Like the prophet we would like to decline the offer: "Ah no, not I, Lord! I am only a child with little understanding!" But our encounter with God drives us on imperiously.

The Catholic, to be sure, will not speak or act against the expressed prohibition of church authorities. But if he knows that he has truly been encountered by God's summons, he will go right to the borderline-limits in standing up for his experience vis-a-vis church authority. He will always be ready to learn from weightier witness, but he will not be prepared to betray his own conscience. The thrust of the Church's future resides in this. It resides in a revitalized poverty, that is, in a deep, underlying attitude which must of course be embodied in concrete actions.

And in this lies the whole difficulty. Our age is oriented around the concrete and the effective as no other age has been. It wants to see deeds. The dictum of Karl Marx, which says that the important thing is not just to know the world but to change it, plays a decisive role in the consciousness of contemporary man – of young people in particular. If a person does not call us to action and concrete deeds, he has lost the ball game before he begins. In his own way Francis of Assisi was a similar spirit in a similar age. He lived poverty in a wholly concrete way, and people saw him as a reformer accordingly. The way he did it is no longer feasible. What remains still is the attitude which lay behind his actions.

Who would pretend to know in advance what concrete results will flow from this attitude? It cannot be worked out by neat calculation. Many would deny this, for they have set all their hope on precise calculation and planning. They analyze the present-day: i. e., the psyche of the masses, man's collective consciousness, the hopes and desires of the human race. They calculate what is technologically feasible, and set out to make it a reality, and founder on the rocks. Why do they fail? Because man, as an individual and a collective body, is much too complicated. Because opposing forces are always at work in every individual, as Paul of Tarsus pointed out long ago. Because a human being coerced into doing what is good and right would not be a human being at all. Mao wants to coerce people into doing good selflessly. But that is a contradiction in terms. If they do not follow him of their own free will, then they are not selfless; and no one can coerce a person to do something of their own free will. And never will all men do what is good and decent of their own free will.

The most humane state or political community is the one which uses the minimum of force and coercion to get the maximum of selfless dedication to the community out of the individual, utilizing all the social and economic aids that are at man's disposal. Insofar as coercion is concerned, the goal of the state must be to make itself superfluous as far as possible.

The duty of the Church, as the community of those called to freedom in Jesus Christ, must be to take the lead in living the stage of freedom attainable at a given moment within her own sphere. Her members must try to present this goal effectively to the world. That presupposes unheard of mobility on the part of the Church, if she does not want simply to propose demands that no one will take seriously. She must also show mobility in her own ecclesial operations, structures, and activities. She must also show mobility in her life and activity relating to the world.

Today people admit that the trend of evolution and development in some respects is pointing towards a diminution of man's freedom – because of the applied sciences in particular. More and more planning is inevitable. There is a real danger that the individual will be totally lost in the human collectivity. Ever increasing numbers of human beings are living together on the same planet, and this entails more and more classification and ordering of the individual without any freedom of personal decision on his part. He is manipulated, undoubtedly. The immanent laws of economics or technology seem to demand it!

This trend is also operative in the Church, as Pope Paul VI indicated at the opening of the third session of Vatican II. The Church is spread out around the world, communication is much easier, and there is more intensive interchange between countries. These factors, along with the rise of a world culture, would call for a centralization and tight-knit organization that was neither possible nor necessary in the first few centuries of the Church's history.

Yet there remains the demand for freedom, for ever greater freedom in fact insofar as man's external possibilities for acting are concerned. And there remains the necessity of doing away with coercion that may have been necessary in an earlier day, and that is possible too. It is a real possibility, even though it may take a different form. On the one hand it may be necessary to work out economic plans on an integrated, worldwide scale; on the other hand, freedom of choice in moving from one occupation to another would become greater. On the one hand it may be necessary to nationalize industries and create huge, united economic spheres, so that small private businesses are forced to disappear. On the other hand, large-scale operations demand team work and a large amount of room for the play of individual initiative on the part of the specialists involved. The dictatorial manager, who rules supreme on his own, is becoming more and more an impossibility.

In a real sense this holds true for the Church as well, insofar as she represents an organization that can be studied by sociologists and that is subject to the laws governing human cohabitation in her process of development. Thanks to her distinctive, evangelical attitude of poverty, the Church is obliged to be more mobile than any other social institution. Not in the sense that she will stand in the vanguard of any and every eccentric movement soon destined to collapse, but in the sense that she will more readily free herself from outdated forms than any other institution.

The person who takes the lead in living this example for her would be the saint of the future. Today more than ever before in the history of the Church, I think it is more likely to be a team of divinely inspired persons rather than a single personality by himself. I do not mean to deny that holiness is always a strictly personal trait. But one of these personal traits is a relationship to others, for the perfection of the individual is possible only within the social dimension. While that was always true, this social dimension can be tangible to a greater or lesser degree. Francis of Assisi wanted a brotherly community that was only minimally bound to "superiors" and "rules," that was underpinned mainly by personal encounter with God and selfless service to others. People say he was no organizer, and therefore he could not help but run aground when his community grew into the thousands. He died of grief and accepted this fate as the cross of Christ.

But it could just as well be that his age was not yet ripe or mature enough to realize his goal. Who would say that our age is not mature enough to better implement and carry out what was impossible then? So the holy figure stands once again on the hillside, in the dawning light of a new age. But now it is no longer a single individual, but a group of men. Now their garb is not beggarly clothes but radical detachment from everything that must be defended by force, and a resounding appeal to the goodness of man who was made in God's image.

5. Francis, the Revolutionary

It has become the order of the day to connect the words "Christian" and "revolutionary," "revolution" and "Christianity," with one another. For many, of course, that is still a tabu. For centuries it was impossible for a Christian to be a revolutionary. He could not be a revolutionary in the temporal sphere because the reigning authority had been established by the grace of God and the resultant regime was sacred. He could not be a revolutionary in the ecclesiastical sphere because the Church had been founded by God himself.

But let us not kid ourselves here. How many revolutions have taken place in the course of history! How quickly the Church has managed to reconcile herself to their outcome! That holds true even for the French revolution, which certainly overturned the foundations of the whole social and political structure. And look what has happened in the Church itself! There is no denying that if Peter or Paul came back today, they would have a hard time recognizing the Church of Christ that they had proclaimed when they took a look at its present pattern: e. g., its structures, its laws, and even its dogmas.

So something has certainly happened, and one can hardly picture it as a harmonious development from bud to blossom. Pope John XXIII, always the history professor, could only smile at those who pictured it so. The fact that change has taken place in the social or ecclesial realm does not of itself constitute a revolution, even though the change may be a significant one for the moment.

What, then, makes the revolutionary to be such? Many believe it is a matter of attitude. One party chose to call the existing situation into question, the other party chose to keep it as it had been. Vatican II proclaimed that the Church is ever on the road towards its goal but has not yet reached it: not only because she continually falls away from her ideal and must be brought back to it again – which is certainly true, but also because the course of history continues to move forward and changes keep occuring in the social, economic, and scientific realm. Hence the pattern of the Church, which resides in the world and shares its life, must continually change its shape and language without giving up the Church's identity or the truth entrusted to her. Vatican II spelled all this out more clearly than it had ever been done before, and many see that as a summons to permanent revolution. They are writing books on the "theology of revolution." In harsh terms they describe the attitude of Christ vis-a-vis the establishment attitude of the Jewish religious authorities. And they are critical of Paul for urging Christians to accommodate themselves to the world, for to them the "world" is the embodiment of the desire to remain frozen in the structures of an immutable order. As they see it, the Church must do more than engage in the indirect tactics of political theology whereby the Church as well as the individual Christian candidly and publicly criticizes and offers protests against the state regime. They demand a permanently revolutionary attitude from the Church in the temporal sphere as well; it follows from the eschatological attitude that the Christian should have.

Now these people would be right, if revolution is in fact the same thing as a perduring stance of calling things into question, as a perduring awareness of the fact that we are nomadic wayfarers who must always be prepared to fold up our tents and move on. But is that what revolution means?

It seems to me that such an attitude can be called "revolutionary" only when it involves a situation where any and every alteration of the existing order is opposed and rejected by those in power. But where do we find such a situation? Basically, nowhere in fact. In reality the problem is of a different nature. Consider the situation with the Catholic Church, for example. Here no one will deny that there is nothing which is absolutely immutable. No liturgical rite, no structure, no principle of canon law, no dogma is the last immutable word with respect to its formulation. If a person were to deny this, he would be a magician not a Christian. But in fact there are more than a few Christians who believe they are obligated to ground the identity of Christ's church on specific, immutable forms. They will acknowledge that other things can be changed, but even there they prefer to tackle the job with great circumspection. They talk about evolution and reject revolution.

Revolution, they say, *destroys* the hitherto existing forms. That is its first and primary effect. Afterwards, because man cannot live without forms, new ones are created to replace the old ones. Then we no longer have revolution but a new consolidation of forms. By contrast, evolution allows what has already existed to be worked up into a better, future-oriented pattern, without destroying the good features of an earlier day. So, for example, the conception of cosmic evolution moving up to man and beyond him, as depicted by Teilhard de Chardin, shows up as evolution. Whether one agrees with his theses or not, Teilhard de Chardin is certainly not a revolutionary, even when he tears down the theses of anti-evolutionists. For, he tears them down only to put something else in their place.

In this sense neither Copernicus nor Galileo were revolutionaries in the realm of the natural sciences. Copernicus remained a natural scientist. Galileo stepped beyond this boundary by drawing conclusions relating to the religious sphere and demolishing an established Scriptural exegesis without offering a better one in its place. From a religious viewpoint Galileo was a revolutionary. Only later ages managed to find a better Scriptural interpretation. Galileo had no desire to be a revolutionary of course. That explains his retraction and his tragic finale, which is so often depicted in distorted terms.

As far as Jesus Christ himself is concerned, one must say that he did not confront the old covenant and the Judaic law as a revolutionary at all. He willed to "fulfill" it. To be sure, this meant the dropping of many things e. g., the temple, circumcision, many prescriptions dealing with externals. To those who did not regard these things merely as preparatory realities pointing towards the future, who wanted to hold on to these practices, Jesus – the historical Jesus – was a revolutionary. Thus he died as a revolutionary. But at bottom he carried out and fulfilled the dynamic, evolving plan of God. He did not regard himself as a revolutionary.

Or is revolution characterized by the fact that it takes place swiftly and unexpectedly? Is it a sudden and radical change? People say: "That event revolutionized my life." By which they mean that a certain event changed their living habits in a flash, revised their judgment of other people's behavior, and introduced a whole new scale of values. In such a case, however, the person is not really a revolutionary; rather, a revolution happens to him.

The same thing can happen in the social realm. We talk about the "technological revolution." It is indeed the revolution of man, who discovered the technology and made it operational. But he certainly had no notion that this would radically alter his whole way of thinking and his picture of man, that he would no longer feel himself a part of nature and the cosmos, that he would gradually come to see himself as the measure of all things. These results were not part of his plan, and even today we cannot estimate where the "technological revolution" will lead us. We can only be sure that something has happened to us, that we have become different. We have suffered a revolution much more than we have made one.

What I have just said about the "technological" revolution applies even more to what we might call the "Christian" revolution. Its root cause is not some plan or discovery of man. It is God's activity in man, his concrete "yes" to man that was spoken in Jesus Christ. Is it a sudden breakthrough that alters the world in a fundamental way? Well it is sudden insofar as this particular human being, Jesus of Nazareth, appears on the scene at a given moment in history which we can pinpoint historically. His appearance did something which we cannot prove unequivocally in historical terms. It inwardly transformed the lives of all human beings before and after him, *implanting in every creature an orientation towards the kingdom of God.* That is a revolution which is clearly discernible only to faith. It is working itself out in history, to be sure, but not in a clear and compelling way. Yet it is ever present – influencing, suffusing, and insistently changing the behavior of the individual and the structures of society. It is, as it were, an insatiable hunger, a utopia that must be sought unceasingly, a permanent revolution, an Absolute hidden in relative things. Are we right in calling that a revolution?

As we just noted, Christianity entails an orientation towards the kingdom of God. It takes more visible and tangible form in the ever changing cast of political and social structures, insofar as they are geared towards greater humanization, self-determination, and freedom for all without exception on the basis of their dignity as human beings. In the last analysis, they cannot achieve their fulfillment on their own; it must be bestowed on them as a gift. Thus the effect of God's activity in Christ is somehow "on hand" at every revolution – presuming it is not a purely negative, destructive revolution, if there is such a thing. That existential – it colors our whole existence – is the witting or unwitting cry for the kingdom of God. No one can evade it. In revolution it becomes more clearly visible and more concretely felt. Man feels the tug of a current, of a stream more powerful than the immediate thrust of a given local revolution yet sweeping up the latter in its wake.

So the question again: Is Christianity a revolution? Amid the revolution-filled air of our day it is a very topical question that grows more explosive every day. In such an atmosphere, one-sided outlooks and emphases are unavoidable. They *must* be such, because the Greek-inspired humanism of perfect balance and measure on all sides would be a betrayal of man in the concrete, who can escape his distortion only through one-sided counter-moves. If there were no sin, Christ's crucifixion would be a sin. It is "in itself" a one-sided distortion. And the same holds true for world evolution, quite apart form sin. If a person is attuned to the dynamic thrust of evolution and history, he should not be pressured into preserving balance and equilibrium. Here we have the critical difference between classical humanism and the "new" humanism. It also means that the word "revolution" has changed its value-setting. Has Paul VI weighed this fact closely?

Nonetheless, revolution, in the strict sense of the word, applies to the *political* realm; and Jesus Christ does not allow himself to be taken over by politics. There is no denying that he scrupulously kept his distance from the realm of political action, even though there was every inducement to get involved. One may of course object that the concrete situation in which he found himself could well have prevented political involvement. He would have had to immerse himself in an already existing political front, the very spirit of which was contrary to his intentions. He was obliged to keep his distance from it. That is not to say that the attitude he held, which clearly bore an essentially social cast, did not necessarily entail consequences affecting political structures. But it does mean that the message of Jesus did not signify direct intervention in the political aspects and forms of life. It worked at a deeper level. It did not work to change structures directly, thereby changing men's outlook indirectly. It worked in the opposite direction, seeking to change human beings first and then, indirectly, the social and political structures.

Hence both the ecclesiastical state and the state church proved to be unserviceable models for turning the Christian message into a reality. But there remains the duty of the Christian community to evaluate every form of civil government in terms of its fitness for embodying the Christian outlook. Depending on the given concrete situation, this duty must be stressed to a greater or lesser degree. Depending on the possibilities of the concrete situation, the concrete state of people's awareness, the status of science, technology, and everything else that influences and conditions men's lives in common, faith-based criticism of societal and governmental structures will necessarily differ. At times when revolution looms on the horizon – one need only look at South America today – such criticism may turn into a duty. One may be obliget to speak out firmly and unequivocally, even to renounce all ties with those in political power who could put through fundamental changes speedily (i. e., carry out a revolution) but do not do so.

In this respect South American bishops are fully justified in excommunicating – i. e., excluding from the community of the

Church – governmental leaders, police chiefs, and domestic ministers. They are only doing their duty. But as far as I can see, they have only adopted such measures when members of the clergy, who had been fighting for social reforms, were imprisoned, tortured, and expelled from their country. In short: when government authorities violated constitutional rights accorded to the Church.

A similar approach has been evident in Spain recently – in isolated cases, at least. I dont't believe that this limited concern for her own interests is enough. The Church cannot wait until her vested rights are attacked before feeling obliged to protest. Wherever structural reforms are a public necessity, wherever the human dignity of Christians or Non-Christians are being clearly and shamefully violated, there the Church as the symbol of Christ in this world must take a stand on the side of the downtrodden and oppressed, and expel those who do not from her midst. She went about doing this all too hesitantly during the Nazi era. So long as the Church herself was not attacked, she kept silent all too often; or else she fled into non-binding statements of principle that had little serious impact on the concrete situation.

In this way the Church slides, almost by necessity, into the realm of world-building in the positive sense. There arises something like a "Christian" world alongside the "secular" world. It leads to a ghetto-existence, as we have learned only too painfully. It poses great theological dangers, too, because it only too easily misconstrues the work of redemptive grace in all men, including Non-Christians. Or else the Church falls apart in the secular world and allows the witness of Christ to be taken over by politics and societal structures. That is precisely what should not happen, and no shifting of transcendence to some eschatological future will salvage the situation. In the last analysis Christ's message is not only a promise but also a presence. The kingdom of God has already begun!

Only from this starting point, it seems to me, can we approach the issue plaguing people's minds in connection with the term "revolution": *the use of force.* Many people will accord the appellation "revolutionary" only to someone who, at the very least, does not rule out the possibility of using force in his commitment to transform existing conditions. That is extraordinarily astonishing in an age when people are moving towards the abolition of the death penalty everywhere; when people are reacting strongly against the use of force by the police and would like to prohibit them from carrying weapons in some countries (e. g., Italy); when refusal to engage in military service on grounds of conscience is spreading in ever widening circles.

A short few years ago there was no noticeable enthusiasm for the use of force. The horrors of the war still weighed too heavily on everyone. There was Gandhi, who had led a huge nation to freedom through the strategy of non-violence. There was Martin Luther King, Jr., a truly Christian man, proposing the same tactic of non-violence. Despite all the suffering and injustice endured by black people in the United States, he believed in the power of non-violent love. His line of thought was simple and clear. Force begets hate, hate begets hate and force in return. Man is caught in a vicious circle, which can only be broken by the revolutionary power of love. No matter what people did to their homes, their schools, or their person, his followers would answer with love. This response of love would awaken the goodness in their enemies and break the circle of hate, as Jesus himself had pointed out. When his home was bombed in Montgomery and a crowd of angry blacks gathered outside, Martin Luther King, Jr. had this to say:

"If you have weapons, take them home; if you do not have them, please do not seek to get them. We cannot solve this problem through retaliatory violence. We must meet violence with non-violence. Remember the words of Jesus: 'He who lives by the sword will perish by the sword....' We must love our white brothers... no matter what they do to us. We must make them know that we love them. Jesus still cries out in words that echo across the centuries: 'Love your enemies; bless them that curse you; pray for them that despitefully use you.' That is what we must live by. We must meet hate with love" (Martin Luther

King, Jr., *Stride Towards Freedom: The Montgomery Story,* New York: Harper & Row, 1958, pp. 137–38).

He paid for his Christian revolution with his life. But that is not a valid proof against his approach. So did Jesus Christ, who was led like a lamb to the slaughter.

One can and indeed must make a distinction here, noting the situation of countries where intolerable injustice holds sway. A small minority enjoys the comforts of life and maintains structures that make it impossible for the vast majority to lead a decent human existence. They must endure a life-style that does not simply pose great obstacles to personal advancement and improvement but actually leads to subhuman degradation. In such a situation the first use of force does not come from the revolutionaries. It is already present in the forcible oppression.

That is the dismal situation in many areas of Latin America. One need only read the reasons given by Che Guevara and Camilo Torres for resorting to the use of force. When we read their words, we do not find hate but grief. We do not find revolutionary bombast or demagogic talk but rather sober, objective analyses of the real societal situation. From them we do not hear explosive rhetoric, as we do from the ideology-bound revolutionaries in our affluent societies. The latter do indeed carry banners with the names of Che and Camilo Torres on them, but is it possible that they do not appreciate the difference in their situation?

Let me offer two examples to make my point here. Father Manfred Hörhammer, the tireless Capuchin apostle for peace in the spirit of Francis, told me this story about Camilo Torres. He had already opted for armed resistance when he received an unexpected visit from the Secretary General of the International Fellowship of Reconciliation, Jean Goss, and his wife. They both explained their conception of non-violent, Franciscan revolution. Camilo Torres was greatly taken by their presentation. Three days later, when they announced that they had to move on, he urged them to remain for awhile longer: "Stay with us for a month and teach us about non-violent revolution. I think I might be converted to your viewpoint once I come to appreciate how it works." They were not able to stay any longer, however, but that may have been a mistake.

Then there is the case of Ernesto Cardenal, a revolutionary in Nicaragua during the early fifties. He was captured with a gun in his hand, imprisoned, and tortured. Composer of the well known South American Psalms, he was not an armchair revolutionary but a frontline man. Today he lives on an island, not far from his birthplace in Granada, which is inhabited by small farmers and illiterates. With the help of a few friends he has built an elementary school and a modest polyclinic. He wants to keep the farmers from ending up in the slums and *favelas* of the big cities, which ring South America like a crown of misery. Now a Trappist, he wants to put brakes on the unhealthy line of present development from within. But let no one think that he has become apolitical. He himself says: "Politics is still my deep concern, but now I see it differently than I used to." He sees himself as a force of the future imbedded in the society of today. As he puts it:

"The artist has always been completely integrated into society. Not into the society of his own time but into the society of the future. The artist, the poet, the scholar, and the saint are members of the society of the future. This society of the future already exists today, like a seed waiting to bud. Not tied to political boundaries, it is composed of individuals and small groups scattered around the world. Insofar as I am a poet, I am an integral part of this society. Insofar as I am a priest, a pacifist, a Christian anarchist, and a Gandhian in politics, I feel that I am a solid member of this society as well. This society of the future seeks to stand up against the forces of backwards-looking people and to usher in future progress as quickly as possible."

I have deliberately avoided the basic, theoretical question of the use of force and concentrated on the witness of authentic Christians in seemingly inescapable situations. And it seems to me that one can say this: Even in the most extreme situations, violent revolution in the name of Christian witness is a highly questionable, if not totally impossible, action. Now that does not mean that a Christian may not, and as a last resort might not be obliged to, take this course; but if he does take it, then his witness on behalf of the kingdom of God is only indirectly embodied in it. Or, it might be more exact to say that any political revolt, including one that uses force, is a matter for the Christian laity as all political activity is; but it is not the sphere of the Church as a whole. In other words, it is not a matter for the clergy, members of religious orders, and those laity whose vocation in life involves direct service to the Church.

The basis for this twofold division is the twofold aspect of the kingdom of God in our given historical situation: i. e., the fact that it is "already here" and "still to come." Since the appearance of Jesus Christ, the kingdom of God is already present; and its sign is the Church of Christ. The kingdom of God is a kingdom of total love in which God is "all in all." But this kingdom is not yet manifest, not even in the pattern of Christ's Church. So when Vatican II talks about the eschatological character of the wayfaring Church, it has this to say: "Until there is a new heaven and a new earth where justice dwells (cf. 2 Pt. 3,13), the pilgrim Church in her sacraments and institutions, which pertain to this present time, takes on the appearance of this passing world. She herself dwells among creatures who groan and travail in pain until now and await the revelation of the sons of God" (*Lumen gentium,* no. 48).

Thus the laws, offices, and sacraments of the Church, along with many other things, are among those things which "groan and travail" in expectation of God's sons being revealed. This must be made evident in the fact that they are used sparingly, used as "necessary evils" which point towards their own looked-for obsolescence. And along with this goes another basic approach on the part of the Church. Those features of the Church which pay tribute to the "appearance of this passing world," but which are most alien to the real life of God's kingdom, must be eliminated in anticipation of that kingdom – as a "utopian" or, at the very least, representative gesture. As Hörhammer would put it: From a "metahistorical viewpoint" non-violent revolution is the only possible revolution for Christians, the only one they are required to make.

Now what does this very modern and timely discussion have to do with the Poverello of Assisi, who did not live in the age of atomic bombs and terror tactics? Is it not beside the point to bring him into play here? I think not. To be sure, not every gesture and approach of this man, who lived hundreds of years ago, is a model for us to copy today. To be sure, many of the questions which press upon us today had not even been glimpsed on the horizon in his day. But there is another side to the story. First, the "metahistorical" point of view, which is so much a part of being a Christian, became transparent in the figure of Francis as it has perhaps in no other Christian embodiment. Secondly, it can be said without exaggeration that the concrete efforts of Francis to live the gospel took such an explosive form, were so ahead of his time, that they were in fact premature. That is why – and I mean no criticism here – they were modified by the official Church and accommodated to real conditions – even by those who greatly admired the Poverello, such as Cardinal Ugolino, the future Pope Gregory IX. But that does not mean that things must remain so forever. What is premature today may be quite timely tomorrow.

Every religious order must have two constitutions. One exhibits its metahistorical pattern, its inner outlook and spirituality. The other frames this spirituality in juridical forms. The latter constitution must be adapted to its day. The more timely it is in this respect, the sooner it will be out of date. So if the Order was not founded solely to meet a specific need of the day (which has also occurred), then the latter constitution must be changed constantly. And this modification must be all the more frequent and comprehensive (visibly at least), if an age is changing more rapidly on all fronts.

In this lies a real handicap. It is the second constitution, the juridical form, that is given ecclesiastical approval. It is read over and over again, and turned into hallowed ground. It becomes the "holy rule." In practice strict following of the rule is often placed ahead of the gospel and its commands, so that the spirit of the gospel is muffled completely. It happened over and over again in the course of history without anyone finding a proper corrective.

Surely we cannot help but be struck by the fact that we find the barest minimum of such legal codification in the New Testament. Even when it is a question of "divine law," it is not specified so narrowly that it does not allow for different concrete embodiments. That is a daring approach, presupposing great trust and confidence in the power of the Spirit, in spirituality. Despite all the consequences of his Incarnation, the founder of Christianity had such confidence. And the concrete effects were internal debates and splits, which occurred in the very first eras of the Church's existence. I think it is a poor excuse to ascribe this lack of fixed forms in the primitive Church to the people's expectation that Christ's return was imminent. The argument presented by some is that the Lord and his apostles expected Christ's second coming to be very soon, therefore they did not think it necessary to give fixed norms to the early community. But one could argue the exact opposite. A fixed and highly structured organization could have had a powerful effect over the short run; and since only a short time remained before the second coming, one would have expected such an organization to be set up.

But let us bypass that whole question, for the real problem lies deeper. The good news sought to liberate man, to introduce him to the freedom of the sons of God. The stress was clearly on an inner transformation; external forms took a subordinate position. The revolutionary feature of Christianity was embodied in the reversal of emphasis. Even before the Christian changes external forms, he is already a freed man within. In my opinion, one cannot spend enough time pondering why the primitive Church, as Jesus left it, was so poor in fixed forms! All the interpretations which suggest that Christ did not intend to found a Church are off on the wrong track; they do not do justice to the power of the Holy Spirit.

But I am not trying to say that any and all consolidation of the Church into more tightly knit forms is an aberration. While

Christ was certainly no "lawgiver" and one does him no honor with that title, the Church had to assume a more consolidated form as it grew larger. That is in the very nature of the case. Deviation from the ideal model comes in when the forms are taken to be more important than the spirit, when one comes to believe that the forms are the spirit crystallized in a supratemporal pattern. To be sure, there are sacraments and offices in the Church that can be traced back to divine institution, however one may picture that in the concrete. To be sure, there is also a legitimate and necessary church law. But in the process of concrete consolidation there always remains room for adaptation to the signs of the time, for a closer approximation to the mature pattern of the Christian human being.

Now the astonishing thing is that of all the rules of religious orders we possess, the rule of Francis of Assisi is the least like a real rule. This matter, which we have touched upon before, is a very timely issue in an age when there is so much talk about structural reforms in the Church and in religious orders. One need only read one of the countless commentaries on canon law to see how much is in flux there at the present time. To us it seems to be a revolutionary turn of events. Yet it was all there in the work of Francis of Assisi, who simply wanted to live the gospel.

As far as we can tell, the first rule which he proposed to Innocent III (1209) was merely a patchwork of short Scriptural passages. We no longer have this "patchwork," and recent scholarship has given up all attempts to reconstruct it. The important point is that Francis really did not want to go beyond the "rules of conduct" contained in Holy Scripture. That kept him from turning his rule into a sacrosanct shrine, as almost all other religious orders have done to some extent. In his day it was not possible to carry this approach through to the end, but one might well ask whether it is not possible to do that today.

This first rule of Francis was approved, at least orally, by the Pope. It was followed by three later rules. The longer they were, the more the spiritual aspect retreated into the background and the more they came to resemble the second type of constitution mentioned above. So true is this that Hans Urs von Balthasar presents only *two* rules of Francis in the series on great church figures of which he was the editor (*Die grossen Ordensregeln,* 1961, in the series, *Menschen der Kirche*). There we find the longer second rule of 1221, the first still extant, which was really closer to the spiritual side, and the last definitive rule of 1223 (considered the third rule, but actually the fourth). Commenting on them, Laurentius Casutt calls attention to the fact that even the last rule of Francis is considerably different from all the other religious rules in the Church. A host of practical questions relating to conduct are not mentioned at all. So something of the founder's outlook still remains. As Casutt puts it: "Just as the gospel could hardly be called a law book, so Francis did not want to leave a legal commentary to his friars. Laws need not necessarily stand in the way of the spirit, but they often do. The saint knew this. He knew even better that legal norms are superfluous to a large extent where a living, holy spirit is operative."

This observation itself brings Francis of Assisi closer to our age than any other reform-minded saint is. Now I can quote the words of Father Lippert once again, for their meaning will be clearer:

"The organizational principle which leads from Benedict through Dominic and Ignatius to the newer communities seems to have practically exhausted its inner possibilities.... The fundamental newness which is precisely the thing being sought today by countless souls... is to be found only along a completely different line: along the line of the original ideal of Francis. In other words: in the direction of a freely chosen life style and freely chosen bonds of love; in the direction of a life that operates through spontaneous initiative of the self *rather than through great constructs of the will;* in the direction of a truly living and individual personality shaped by its own *inner laws and standards.* If God should someday deign to reveal the Order of the future to his Church... it will surely bear the stamp of Francis' soul and spirit."

Now let us get to a few specific matters. Today we talk a great deal about the transformation of existing structures, the

Picture page 175:
Francis of Assisi is the first person in the history of Christendom to receive the stigmata. However one may wish to explain this phenomenon, it clearly bears historical witness to his extraordinary emotional penetration into the passion of Christ. Not visible in this picture of the desolate mountain area are the "gigantic cracks and fissures" which reminded Francis of the "rocks split asunder" at the time of Christ's death. Viewing this awesome scene, Francis plunged deeper into that bygone day and sought to plumb its mystery.

Cross atop Mount La Verna,
where Francis received the stigmata.

Picture pages 176–177:
In Siena Francis met a young man who was carrying a basket of wild doves to the marketplace. Francis asked that the doves be given to him, saying: "In Holy Scripture the dove is compared to the soul that is filled with faith and humility. You should not let them fall into the hands of cruel men who will kill them." The young man gave him the doves. Francis put them on his lap and spoke to them: "My sisters, my innocent little ones, why did you let yourselves be captured? Come, I will build nests for you." And so he did. The doves took advantage of the nests, paired up, and bore fledglings. But they were as trusting as chicks where the friars were concerned.

View of Perugia.

Picture pages 178–179:
On one occasion Francis, not far from Portiuncula, was walking through the woods and weeping loudly. A pious soul heard him and asked Francis if he was sick or in pain. Francis replied: "I am weeping over the passion of our Lord Jesus Christ. Must I be ashamed to go through the world, weeping aloud over him?"

Woods in the vicinity of the *Carceri* (grottos, not far from Assisi, to which the friars withdrew to pray all day).

Picture page 180:
One evening Francis was walking with Clare towards Assisi. He said: "Sister, have you heard what people have been saying about us?" She said nothing, for she was close to tears. Francis said: "The time has come for us to part, I think. I shall go off on my own and keep track of you from a distance."
"Father," she replied, "when will we see each other again?" It was winter.
"When the roses bloom," Francis replied.
Then something wondrous happened. It seemed as if thousands of roses had suddenly blossomed around them in the juniper bushes. Clare deftly plucked a huge bouquet of them and dropped them into the hands of Francis. "From that day forward, Francis and Clare were never separated again," concludes the popular legend.

A Poor Clare in her cloister.

need for democratization, the decentralization of authority, and the function of service. We deduce the need for such a transformation, which is also making headway in the Church, from man's growing awareness of his own maturity and adulthood. This growing awareness is evident throughout the world, both in developed and underdeveloped countries. It accords completely with man's dignity as a human being, as Father John Courtney Murray tried to explain over the course of many years. After much earnest debate Vatican II finally came to adopt his viewpoint in its declaration on religious freedom *(Dignitatis humanae personae);* for it grounds its argument on this ontological datum, thus going far beyond the traditional arguments based on tolerance. But Father Murray himself admits that this principle could not become operative in the practical order so long as the notion of human dignity was not alive in the consciousness of peoples and nations. This shift in awareness from a patriarchal outlook to a personal focus is a relatively new datum. It has been quite rightly called a revolutionary event in the history of the human spirit. Over the course of centuries it has worked itself out in many different areas, being mixed up with all sorts of deviations in the process. It has been operative in the realm of politics (e. g., the French Revolution) and in the realm of societal relationships (e. g., the revolutions of the working classes). Its impact reaches down to Marxism and to the student riots of today. It is an historical process that is now worldwide in scope.

But one may well be astonished to find this tendency, grounded solely on the religious soil of the gospel, already operative in the work of Francis of Assisi. In the first (still extant) rule we find this maxim: "All the friars without exception are forbidden to wield power or authority, particularly over one another.... No one is to be called 'prior.' They are all to be known as 'Friars Minor' without distinction, and they should be prepared to wash one another's feet." The Franciscans were the first religious not to elect a "Father Abbot." The religious piety of Francis was deeply grounded on God the Father, but he could not find any place for the father-image within his community of friars. There all were brothers, with different functions of service to perform.

Even the "minister general" could be deposed by his own fellow friars, according to Francis. This could not happen ordinarily in the older Orders, which were organized along strictly hierarchical lines (e. g., the Benedictines, the Cistercians, and the Carthusians). Even later the paternal image continued to play an important role for the Jesuits: e. g., when the duties of various superiors are described in their constitutions. But there is no direct or indirect suggestion of the father-son relationship when relations between superiors and subordinates are described in the Franciscan rule of 1221 or that of 1223 (the one which was solemnly approved by Pope Honorius III).

My feeling is that not enough attention has been paid to this fact. In an age when people's conceptual structures were still sociologically tied up with patriarchal models to a greater or lesser extent, it was an astonishing and indeed revolutionary departure. And it is readily apparent that it was not just a matter of terminology as far as Francis was concerned. He wanted to give expression to an attitude that was meant to differentiate clearly his community from other Orders! And an attempt to explain it away psychologically, by saying that the encounters between young Francesco and his father destroyed his father-image, falls apart in the light of his spirituality. Lacking a deep-rooted awareness of God as his Father, he would have had no grounds for his cosmic mysticism and his love of nature. But the father-image was reserved for God alone. All others are brothers and sisters. The equality of all human beings is taken quite seriously. That is fine and good in terms of the gospel. But in the sociological structures of the medieval period it could not be carried through with complete success.

The case is different today. This line of thought is wholly in accord with the outlook of modern man. When *Paris Match* polled a sampling of young people between eighteen and twenty-five, it found that seventy percent of them had a deep sense of responsibility for the world at large. As they saw it, the meaning of life was to be "useful to others." The common task, shared by all, is what holds the world together in their eyes. And this task is not so much to make scientific progress or to win mastery over the earth and nature, even though these things are indispensable means to the real end. But the real end is the establishment of a fraternal community between all human beings.

Here is the source of the anti-authoritarian attitude evinced by young people. They see authority as a force which creates and maintains inequalities that go against man's dignity, which fails to recognize the equality of all human beings. They do not reject order and structure as such, insofar as these things are solidly grounded on reality; indeed they take these things for granted as necessary presuppositions. What they oppose is not authority as such, but authority which violates man's dignity. Real progress means using science, technology, and the communications media to make it possible for mankind to effectively recognize the dignity of every individual, and to allow each person to contribute his effort to the common good in a free and responsible way. When each person is able to develop his sense of personal responsibility to the utmost, he will help to create the longed-for community among men. The reduction and abolition of coercive structures, along with the shouldering of greater personal responsibility, is the goal of young people. It is the thrust of evolutionary development in our time. The "establishment" comprises all those forces which will not dismantle coercive structures or build new structures because of their narrow, vested interests.

Young people enjoy a certain advantage, for they tend to underestimate the difficulties of any undertaking. They feel the upward rush of life and the great promise it contains. They tear down obstructions without a second thought, failing to realize that such obstructions may also serve as dams to protect the good things. They have not yet come to experience the truth of the parable of the wheat and the chaff, the close-knit intermingling of good and evil which does not allow for thorough weeding. That is certainly true of young people. On the other hand, prudent and cautious people often fail to see that a situation has changed, that unsuspected new possibilities, directions, and insights lie in front of them. So while we may not want to say yes too quickly to all the details and concrete embodiments of the new outlook on life, we should take serious note of the authenticity of the basic underlying tendency. It embodies the hope of the future. If a person blocks and frustrates it with overcautious restrictions, then he is a murderer of mankind – far more so than the treacherous moraines that lie at the edge of glaciers.

If a person has taken a stance against the revolutionary tendencies of the present day, then he should seriously contemplate the figure of Francis. Francis did not infringe upon any authority. On the contrary, he sought approval of his community from the Pope and he asked a Cardinal to be the protector of his Order. So, one might say, he was not a revolutionary after all. But he was. In its *de facto* pattern, his community was a revolution. All were brothers; there was no father in it. There was no specified set of rules. The Spirit was to create new forms as the situation called for them. Francis fashioned a *de facto* revolution without any polemics.

The priests of his day had grown quite corrupt. Some had grown hungry for power; others had become very worldly. Yet he respected them, chose not to preach without their permission, and respectfully kissed their hand in honor of their office. Seemingly a naïve thing to do; in fact, a very realistic approach.

One cannot validly counter this statement by saying that the father-image soon showed up quite forcefully in the structures of the various Franciscan communities, so that they were no longer distinguishable from other religious communities in their type of government. To be sure, the Conventuals used a great deal of gruesome paternal force in dealing with the Spirituals. But that sort of approach stands in dialectical contrast to the real core of the Franciscan approach, as borderline phenomena often do. One cannot pass judgment on the movement solely on that basis. Consider the case of celibacy lived for the sake of the kingdom of God. It is foolish to denigrate this kind of life by saying the person's aggressive drives, repressed by such a life, can easily flow over into a hunger for power. The fact is not to be denied. But if you seek a life-style without any risks, you will not accomplish much at all. It will be a flat existence. The point applies to the Franciscan approach as well.

Moreover, I must say that something of the pervading spirit

of brotherhood continues to live on in the Franciscan communities of today, particularly among the Capuchins. It keeps superiors close to their brother religious in the community. That spirit is quite palpable to an outsider. The spirit of Francis, kept alive in the tone of the rule, is stronger than the spirit of canon law – especially where the latter is merely a formal shell.

Let me get back to the main point. I think we can make this general statement. There are figures in history that bring to light the slumbering forces in a developing thrust. I am thinking, for example, of figures who stand at the dawn of a new era. The age in which they live feels, more intuitively than consciously, that some sort of hidden guiding image for it is being brought out into the open. It rejoices to see this, and becomes almost intoxicated with the insight. But reflective people and realists shake their heads over such utopian dreams. They are right to some extent, but not completely at all. True enough, the new forces have not yet grown to maturity. They are like blades of grass, not yet capable of casting a protective shadow or providing a nest for the birds of the air. So the figures submerge once again, flitting away like a dream. But the new forces continue to grow while older forces, which once held the field, die out. Now, in the hubbub of full-fledged transformation, we must turn our thoughts back to the figure that was there at the start of it all. For now it may be feasible for people to carry through; now it may help us to interpret correctly the "signs of the time." And I use the latter term in the sense of John XXIII and Paul VI, not just in a general sense. Shortly after Vatican II, there was hardly an allocution in which Paul VI did not urge the faithful to explore the "signs of the time."

It would indeed be enough if we paid attention to this one revolutionary feature of Francis. But there is a second aspect which could have just as great an impact. Today when we look at Francis and his first followers in social terms, we tend to see them almost exclusively as a mendicant community. Pledged to poverty, they went about begging. That is how we see them, as far as I can make out. The first thing the new member did was to distribute all his goods to others. From then on he would live off the alms of other people. Such a community is called a mendicant order even today. Its basic foundation is a life of begging, of living off the alms of others, which was recognized at the start as an ideal and virtuous way of life by the Christian community. And even though man soon found ways to make this kind of life tolerable and "reasonable," to take away the sting of privation, that basic foundation has perdured.

This aspect was heightened by the Franciscans insofar as the community as a whole, like the individual, was not to possess anything. But people managed to get around that too, by putting everything into the hands of lay people. They owned the cloisters, the assets of the community, the books and clothes and food. It was indeed one way of breaking out of the social isolation of the cloistered life and establishing contact with the world. And it should not be underestimated, even though virtue lay more on the side of the lay people who agreed to take care of the business of the Order without being paid for it.

Today social circumstances have changed greatly. Then, too, it was shameful to be a beggar; but beggars did make up a recognized social class as they still do in some countries today. On the whole, however, we regard this social relationship as an unsatisfactory one. They should either be provided with jobs, or else the state has an obligation to provide for them. In other words, what was once regarded as a social duty to be fulfilled by the charity of the private individual, is now regarded as a duty of the community as a whole. The beggar today stands as an accusation against the community; it is not doing its duty. Today all religious orders with vows of poverty must ask themselves how this evangelical counsel can be an authentic and comprehensible sign of the kingdom of God in our time. It surely is possible, even in our performance-oriented society.

But if we take a closer look at Francis of Assisi, we will be in for a big surprise. We will find that he did not rest content with asking his friars to live a life of beggary alone. Rather, he bade them to work. Every friar was to work: i. e., to help other people by working in the fields, or tending the sick, or caring for lepers. To be sure, one of the reasons Francis gave for this was the same one that older Orders had given: "Idleness is the devil's workshop." It is an ego-centered reason, and it did not matter to the early desert fathers whether they engaged in basket-weaving or something else. They would put something together one day and take it apart the next. Occupational therapy!

For Francis, however, work meant service to one's neighbor. In his *Testament* he says that every friar should master some handicraft. If the friar does not know one when he enters the Order, then he is to be taught one. And even though the friar is to be poor in dress and possession, he should have adequate tools for his craft. The social aspect of work comes clearly to the forefront with Francis of Assisi. The friar is to take for himself only as much as he needs to live on. The road to riches is closed off to the Franciscan cloister. Pay may be accepted only to meet an immediate need. Only when work brings in nothing may one have recourse to begging. It is a substitute only, and its social aspect is the main thing, i.e., it appeals to the generosity of the other person. There is a deeply revolutionary element in all this, which could be of great use in reforming the notion of "evangelical poverty" today – not just among the Franciscans either.

There is something else to be noted in Francis' notion of work. For him it is not work within a cloistered community; it is work *with and for others.* When we realize that Francis did not want walled cloisters but "places" where six to ten friars lived together, we see in him an openness to the world and a sense of responsibility towards it that is only now being matched by other Orders in their movement toward communes. The basic, underlying thought is this: *living example* is more effective than the words of any sermon where Christian witness is concerned. But such example may have less power to convince people when it is lived in the isolation of a special community with special living conditions that cannot be easily translated to other life-situations. Its power grows stronger, the more clearly and closely the relationship is between the one giving the example and the one who is supposed to benefit from it.

It is regrettable that the Franciscans soon gave up the concrete implementation of this principle. Great convents and houses of study arose. Preaching activity left no time for working with and for others. Apparently they did not see clearly the future-oriented significance of immersion in the surrounding world. Francis did and resisted the trend things were taking as best he could. In my opinion, that is how he would have reacted to any work undertaken as the "special" task of the Order. Today, however, efforts to immerse Christian witness in the life of the surrounding world are the order of the day. They are taken to be revolutionary. But they signify an attempt to overcome the dualism of nature and grace, of the temporal and the spiritual; to take seriously the Incarnation of Christ, which is supposed to be carried forward in the Church.

To be sure, other people are taken aback when they see nuns doffing their religious habits in order to break down the distance between them and their pupils. They think we are going downhill when someone like Father Lombardi in Italy lets all kinds of religious into his Center for a New World; when religious orders let more and more lay people get involved in their work and even take charge of it; when priests enter a secular profession and exercise it as others do. They have no inkling that it all began with the ingenuous Poverello of Assisi.

Of course one can object that there is a risk involved in tearing down protective walls that were built on the basis of long experience. But Francis knew that too. He saw the dangers and took account of the risk of scandal and defeat. But he calmly answered this objection in the words of Jesus himself: "Behold, I am sending you out as sheep in the midst of wolves." That is why his friars were to "expose themselves and their bodies" to enemies seen and unseen. For Francis, in short, risk was an essential component of Christianity. Trusting in the Lord, whose message he wished to live, the friar took on the risk entailed. Is it by chance that the gospel passage about the sheep and the wolves was stricken from the last rule, the one over which the prudent protector of the Order, Cardinal Ugolino, had the final say? Is it that he preferred to trust in human prudence, even though that could not keep off the wolves either?

What Francis wanted to do was to get *Christianity* on the

move, and not just through the intermediation of his community of friars. One is disappointed when he first reads Francis' *Letter to All the Faithful* (1219), his *Letter to the Rulers of the People*, or the oldest *Rule of the Third Order* (1223). Nothing special or revolutionary strikes our eyes. No great program of action is spelled out. We find modest guidelines for prayer and spiritual exercises, and complicated prescriptions for fasting. It gives us the impression that we are dealing with a pious community rather than with a movement inspired by a deep social awareness. Indeed that is how many people see the Third Order even today. We feel sure that the hand of Cardinal Ugolino was deeply involved here, that the "rules" took over the "movement" from the start. But three things are worth noting:

(1) The Eucharist is interpreted as the central Christian happening, oriented towards the life of the community and towards concrete deeds. In his *Letter to a General Chapter* he writes: "In the places where the friars live, only one Mass a day (is to) be said in the rite of the Holy Church." Granting that there is some debate about the kind of Mass being referred to (the longer community Mass only, or private Masses too), it is clear that here we find an emphasis on community participation which was lost afterwards and has only come back into the spotlight in recent years.

(2) Some of the minor prescriptions, whose import we do not yet appreciate today, contributed pointedly to a social transformation in the society of that day. For example, there is the prohibition against bearing arms or pledging them to battle. While one might think it was a matter of external formalities, it brought the members of the Third Order into conflict with rulers all over Europe. Joseph Bernhart points out that it was a "blow to the heart of feudalism." Rulers grasped the revolutionary thrust of this outlook and spoke of it as *rebellion!* Father James Meyer pointed out the reason:

"The Third Order spread so rapidly that some twenty years later a sycophant of Frederick II complained there was scarce a man or woman anymore who did not belong to it. Figure it out: man power available to the mischief-makers was presently at such a premium that they sought by appeals to authority or by main force to press the world turned Franciscan into their service. Then the Church stepped in on behalf of the tertiaries as being her special wards; and at that time, to turn upon the Church was to cut yourself off from life. The mischief adjusted itself gradually to fade out, like the stars before the sun" (*Social Ideals of St. Francis,* 2nd rev. edn., St. Louis and London, 1948, p. 37).

(3) Pervading the whole rule is an earnest concern to establish *peace.* Some people might feel that is just the opposite of revolution. But it is not in a world where feuds and skirmishes are the normal state of affairs. It is a revolutionary concern, presupposing *one* condition: that when the strife is over, one does not restore the same state of affairs which previously led to strife. Francis frequently brought about peace in temporal affairs. And in his book, *Politische Heilige* (1953), Gilbert Kranz points out that Francis never "restored matters to their earlier state; instead he creatively fashioned something better in its place." That was the case in Arezzo and Bologna. In Perugia his efforts failed, and the result was a gruesome blood-bath as he had predicted. We do not know whether he was responsible for the "eternal covenant" in Assisi or not. This Magna Carta says nothing about him being involved. But even though the main reason for it was probably the critical situation of weak Assisi vis-a-vis strong Perugia, it established relationships of a democratic cast which clearly corresponded with Francis' respect for the dignity of the individual. For it freed the serfs, put villagers on an equal footing with the townspeople, and established greater concord between the nobles and the middle class.

Structural changes in society itself were clearly involved here. They loomed in the air. Each class stood over against the other classes. Hostility brewed between nobleman, middle-class merchant, and the propertyless. One cannot say that Francis drew up a new societal model and then tried to implement it. But he did contribute much to such a development. He preached peace. His greeting to everyone was: "Peace be with you." He placed great stress on the fact that this was to be the greeting uttered by all his followers. His radical line of conduct proved that it was not a matter of mere words. He confronted people directly, candidly discussing his faults and theirs.

All this is captured in the strange and obviously symbolic story of the wolf of Gubbio. The two fronts were frozen in opposition. The marauding conduct of the wolf (i.e., the robber knight) fostered anxiety and fear. It seemed that his repressive measures could only be extirpated by an armed rebellion. The modern reader thinks automatically of the situation in Latin America, of people like Che Guevara, Camilo Torres, and Fidel Castro. But Francis tackled the problem differently. He did not exhort the townspeople to take the matter lying down; but neither did he have recourse to armed revolt. He did something much more radical. He left the town unarmed. Everyone thought it was a completely crazy thing to do. It would surely lead to capture, torture, and death. But Francis went anyway and spoke flatteringly to the wolf. He accused him openly of his misdeeds: "You are a robber and despicable murderer; you deserve to be put to a terrible death." It was not a threat, just the plain truth. This immediately took away the wolf's anxiety that lay hidden behind his repressive methods. For the actions of the wolf stemmed from "his hunger of grim savagery." Being "frighteningly big," he could do nothing. Francis promised the wolf that no one would punish him or persecute him. In return, the wolf must not hurt anyone. And what is more, the wolf would be fed every day by the people.

We do not know the historical background of this legend. But one can see in it all the features of Francis' work for the cause of peace. That is its historical kernel.

My feeling is that the Third Order could continue to have as strong an impact today as it did in the twelfth and thirteenth century, if it took the story of the wolf of Gubbio as the guiding principle of its activity. To be sure, it would also have to have its founder's feel for justice, his courage and spirit and faith-inspired imagination. Once upon a time it did have those qualities, and they enabled the Third Order to become a world force in ways that astounded both rulers and ecclesiastical authorities. In modern times various popes – Leo XIII, Benedict XV, Pius XI

– put high hopes on the Third Order for bringing about a renewal of social and economic life. These hopes have not been fulfilled, and one may well ask why. It seems to me they were not fulfilled because attention was focused all too exclusively on one's personal life and the moderate use of worldly goods, and all too little on concern for other people. By concern for other people I mean concern to establish ties of solidarity with those who are oppressed and whose human dignity is being violated. I mean concern to appeal to the conscience of others by one's own example and one's candid criticism, even as Francis appealed to the conscience of the wolf.

Such conduct from a broad spectrum of lay people could represent a revolution today, even more than it did in the twelfth century. The pope was right in that respect. But who is making that kind of revolution today? In the United States the job was entrusted to Martin Luther King, Jr., and he was then left to go it alone. In South America we hear this appeal being voiced by Archbishop Helder Camara. In Africa voices in the churches of Rhodesia speak out against Ian Smith and his regime in Salisbury. Even Non-Catholic newspapers are saying that a stronger front is evident here than that presented by the United Nations, the London government, and violent revolutionary movements.

Such action is unbloody. Is it the same as absolute pacifism? However much some have tried, one cannot place Francis in that particular front. Why? To begin with, because any and every ideology was alien to him, as we pointed out earlier. Did he ever pass judgment on the Crusades? I know of no instance where he did. He spent time among the Crusaders. He reproved them vigorously for their wanton life. But he never passed judgment on the Crusade as such. He himself, of course, did not resort to weapons. He pushed on unarmed to visit the sultan, winning the latter's respect but not his conversion. One cannot possibly depict Francis or his companions as soldiers of war. Yet he did not contest the right of political rulers to take up arms. He had a lasting impact on social and economic life, but he never became a politician.

The distinction seems to be important. It is not just that he distinguished between a person and his office, reproving a person for administering his office badly but never impugning the office itself. He also sharply distinguished his vocation from that of the secular office-holder: "I have no desire to be a landed nobleman, dispensing punishment as political rulers do." He wrote a letter "to all magistrates and consuls, to all judges and governors all over the world." But in it he only urged them not to lose sight of the eschatological vision as they went about their work of building the world. In his letter "to all the faithful" he urged the judge never to ignore mercy or to forget humaneness towards his fellow human beings.

In practice it came down to this. Wherever humanity was being violated, Francis felt obligated to step in. To that extent politics was subject to his judgment. But it was not his thing to engage in positive politics, in the sense of making rational decisions as to how life should be arranged in detail. Yet he was also convinced that the Franciscan spirit could be embodied in a life in the world. He did not picture the Third Order as a confraternity of friars. Indeed, at first it was not called an "Order." It was for the "Brothers and Sisters of Penance" living in their own homes. It was to provide instruction in Christian living to all the faithful. Walter Nigg was quite right when he said: "The Third Order played an essential role in bridging the gap between the religious and secular way of life." And Van den Borne calls it "an integral part of the whole Franciscan movement."

That whirls us once again into the maelstrom of change taking place in our day. In the early days of the Third Order, shallow-minded people talked about "making monks out of the laity." Today they talk about "the laicization of the monk." Both are wrong. What is involved here is a tension essential to every Christian, which shows up in two social expressions. Neither of the two would be meaningful by itself. Each contains something of the other in itself, just as every man has feminine traits in himself and every woman has masculine traits in herself; that does not take away the tension existing between the two. The Poverello of Assisi was the first to glimpse this fact and flesh it out in a revolutionary way.

One final point should be added here that seems essential to the character of the Franciscan revolution. There is no doubt that Francis wanted to reform the clergy and the hierarchy as well. He said quite frankly: "First I want to convert the prelates of the Church in humility and reverence." Let no one suggest that he did not recognize the depravity of the clergy and higher circles in the Church. He was not the ingénue which many would like to make of him. But he did not entertain any idea of mobilizing public opinion against those clergymen, from the lowest to the highest, who were greedy for money and power, who used their power to shore up the authority of the Church by despotic means and claimed that they were doing it to uphold the authority of God. Although their conduct was a public scandal, he never publicly exposed them to ridicule.

Was that in line with the general outlook of his day, which of course served as the framework for his own consciousness? No indeed! That century was filled with the accusations hurled by penitential preachers at the vices and scandalous behavior of prelates. The criticism of today's publicists seems mild by comparison! And one cannot maintain that the publicists of the twelfth century – which is what preachers were – did not know the power of public opinion or were not able to use it in a purposeful way. With it they stirred up broad-based popular movements, obstinate disobedience of staid authority, and even bloody insurrections here and there. The Waldensian crusade got under way as the Franciscan Order was being founded (1209/1210), and it had not yet ended when Francis died.

No matter what one tries to make of it, the fact is that Francis resolutely rejected the pathway of violent opposition and disobedience to ecclesiastical authority. For him that was "not Catholic" and, in the last analysis, contrary to the gospel. His attitude is astonishing, for Francis was certainly no *formalist*. When one fasting friar broke down from hunger, Francis sat down and ate with him to his heart's content, so that the friar would not feel ashamed of himself. Once Francis even broke into a stranger's vineyard and happily joined a crestfallen friar in eating the stranger's grapes. The blows he received from the owner of the vineyard did not upset him at all. He gave away the only Bible the friars possessed to a poor woman, so that she might buy bread. When too many pilgrims had come to Portiuncula and friar Peter Catanii wanted to accept money from the well-to-do in order to buy food for the rest, Francis rejected the suggestion and said: "Take the cloth and ornaments from the altar of the Blessed Virgin and sell them, if you have nothing else to relieve the situation.... God will surely send someone who will give back to his Mother what we needed." When Francis lay dying and his loyal Jacoba, a distinguished lady from Rome, came to visit him, he remarked that the rule about cloistered seclusion did not apply where she was concerned: "How kind and generous of her to come so far to see me!" In his rule we read that "need knows no law." He was quick to point to the example of David, who ate the bread on display in the temple when he was fleeing from his persecutor.

On the other hand, he reiterated repeatedly that he would never preach in the district of a bishop or pastor without that person's permission, even when that person was leading an evil life. Some people present such examples to show that authority was sacred to Francis. It certainly was. But Francis knew very well that a command running counter to conscience was invalid, and it was his conscience that bade him to preach. Why then did he not make a distinction between the legitimate and the illegitimate commands of authority, as others did?

Many explanations are offered in the literature on Francis. People point to his distinction between the person and his office, his evident reverence for the ordained priest, his feel for proper social order. All these things can be documented, but I don't believe they explain the matter fully and satisfactorily. One must add the fact that Francis wanted to unleash a revolution, a revolution based on the gospel, and violent opposition did not fit into his notion of that kind of revolution. Why? Because, in my opinion, the starting point for his revolution was an appeal to man's freedom. No one was excluded here, not even those who held power. Had he broken the power of church men by forceful means, he would have been on the wrong side. Like them, he would be using means that the founder of the Church had not envisioned for the spread of the gospel. He would be trying to anticipate the eschatological day in a precipitate way. And if he managed to succeed in this, power would have merely changed hands. People would still entertain the illusion that the gospel should be preached by means of force.

Let me cite a few texts that make this point clear. In the *Legend of the Three Companions* (compiled by John of Ceprano), we find statements which Francis was wont to make to his friars at the annual general chapters (on Pentecost and September 29). Talking about the attitude of friars towards priests, Francis is quoted as giving them the following admonition:

"He exhorted the friars not to pass judgment on anyone, not even on those who dress in finery and live in luxury. He said: 'God is lord over us and them. He can send out his call to them, and justify those whom he has called' (cf. Rom. 8,30). Francis wanted his friars to approach such people with reverence as their brothers and lords. 'They are *our brothers* insofar as they have the same Creator that we do. They are *our lords* because they help good people to practice penance and purification and provide them with the necessary means for persevering. The demeanor of the friars among men should be such that all who hear and see them feel a holy urge to bless and praise God. If you preach peace with your lips, you should carry it in your heart even more. No one should be roused to indignation or anger by you. Your modesty should incite all to peace, meekness, and harmony. *For we are called to heal the wounded, to bind up the disabled, and to set aright those who have gone astray.* Many who now seem to be children of the devil, *will become disciples of Christ some day.*'"

We find an even more Christ-like thought in the *Mirror of Perfection.* When some of the friars ask Francis to get permission from the Pope to preach everywhere without having to depend on the permission of the local bishop, who often made them wait for it, Francis replies with a sharp reprimand:

"You are Friars Minor, and yet you do not perceive the will of God. Yet get in my way, when I am trying to win the whole world for God the way he wants it to be done. First I will win over the rulers of the Church through humility and reverence. When they see our holy way of life and our humble reverence, they will beg us to preach and proclaim penitence. This approach will bring people to our preaching better than any of your privileges; the latter will only make you arrogant."

And in Francis' *Testament* we read these harsh words:

"In virtue of obedience I strictly forbid the friars, wherever they may be, to petition the Roman Curia, either personally or through an intermediary, for a papal brief, whether it concerns a church or any other place, or even in order to preach, or because they are being persecuted. If they are not welcome somewhere, they should flee to another country where they can lead a life of penance, with God's blessing."

Here Francis draws a sharp and clearcut line of division between the Franciscan method of changing the world and the method of the Curia in those days. The indirect criticism is unmistakable. But it is so unobtrusive and genteel that we today might be reluctant to label such an approach as revolution. Yet it changed the life of society and the Church as none of the revolutions employing force ever did. To be sure, the impetus flagged. Even while Francis was still alive, the seeds of destruction were being sown in it – by his friend, Cardinal Ugolino, the protector of the Order, and by all too prudent friars like Elias of Cortona, his vicar and later his successor as head of the Order.

Francis clearly saw the danger and felt its deadly sting. He literally cried out aloud against it, but he was not led to resort to forceful means as a last resort. Some might say: He was no fighter. I would maintain the opposite: He stuck to his evangelical reform and revolution right down to his death. The stigmata with its five wounds are merely the external, visible sign of his continued obedience to the pathway which he saw as the pathway of the gospel. And so he died, like his Master; and that, too, is an essential and decisive component of this type of revolution.

Now I will not try to go back to the theoretical questions discussed at the beginning of this chapter. I will not attempt to draw any basic, theoretical conclusions that would determine why and to what extent armed revolution, the forceful toppling of structures that have become impassable, can be permissible or prohibited to the Christian. The reckoning would never work completely. But it is my opinion that we are forced to this twofold conclusion in practice. On the one hand, those who believe they must wage such revolutions are not to be turned into devils. On the other hand, today as long ago the Christian promise lies with those who struggle to follow the Franciscan pathway of humble example, fully aware of the fact that in practice it brings its followers to the cross. They will commit themselves wholly to the work of building new social structures; and they will flesh out this goal where they can. Again today they will be persecuted, tortured, and thrown into prison. They will appear to be the most foolish of utopians, and they will appear to go under without having any impact. But even here in our little interval of time, their example and their harsh but humble appeal to man's generosity will contribute more to social change and structural renewal than all the boisterous proponents of armed revolution. And the reason is simply that God has deigned to show us that his weakness is stronger than the powerful of this world. It is not something to be proved. It is the folly and scandal of the Cross. It is the wisdom of God which alone wins out.

6. Noblesse

In the chapters of this book I have talked about the childlikeness of Francis; about the gospel and his ideology-free style of thought; about poverty as an appeal to generosity; and about revolution, or the will to change the world. In doing this I have moved from two different directions.

On the one hand, I have started from present-day questions and then taken a look back at the figure of the Poverello who lived eight centuries ago. It became clear that despite all the differences and time-conditioned factors evident in the great preachers of salvation, the essential traits remain the same. In their temporal pattern they make visible and transparent a transcendent, supratemporal reality. In this sense all of them, individually and collectively, are answers to our present-day questions. They are so in a negative sense inasmuch as they indicate that many of the answers, towards which certain trends would compel us, are blind alleys and dead ends. They are so in a positive sense inasmuch as they provide us with a divining rod to seek out the real, authentic wellsprings; for they only register a reaction there.

On the other hand, I have started with an analysis of Francis himself. His distinctive character was bound up with the landscape that comes through almost unchanged in the pictures of this book. It was also bound up with his point in time. In part that age is dead or dying. In part it signified a new beginning whose forces are only now coming to full flower and filling us with breathless hope and anxiety. This analysis of Francis has shown us something astonishing. It has confirmed that Francis, in his character and concrete life, somehow *did not fit into* his age. He towered above it, filling it with fright and anxiety, because he conducted the most radical and, at the same time, the most peaceful campaign against the establishment of his time. It was the establishment of consecrated power, embodied first and foremost in money, but also in weaponry and theological systematization. In his own age he could not help but suffer defeat. He was laid low "with good reason" by his own well-meaning friends and friars. Unarmed, he allowed himself to go down to defeat, even though he did raise his voice to complain. The song of triumph which broke from his lips on his deathbed is something which can be understood and realized only today!

So I have moved from two directions, as I said before. And despite the inadequacy of these considerations, and the initial chagrin they may have caused to the reader, they may have helped many to see that Francis was really born for our present age – eight hundred years ago. That is how deep his roots are. They had to be, for they were to produce a very tall tree that could withstand many storms.

But as I look over these considerations and comparisons, there seems to be something missing in what I have said about him here, something that constitutes his magnificence. Did I allow myself to be taken over by the burning questions of the present day, so that I distorted his image? Have I added something extra to the mysterious and primal ground of his personality, which is alien to our age, when it is precisely that primal ground that still draws thousands to Assisi out of homesickness and nostalgia? Feelings of nostalgia would mean that we no longer possess this primal ground but that it is part of our heritage and roots, that we long to go back to it as we stand in alien territory. It would mean we are alienated and frustrated in and despite all our progress.

In Chapter 2, where I spoke of the child that Francis was deep down, I tried to allude to this point. That was all right, and I will not retract anything I said there. But that may not have been precisely the central core. So here at the end I must take another go at it.

In 1965 Erich Rohr finished a book on Francis entitled *Der Herr und Franziskus*. This Franciscan had spent fifty years studying Francis and was eighty-one at the time. When he died almost exactly a year later, the book was published under the editorship of Kajetan Esser, another Franciscan who is an eminent scholar on Francis. In Rohr's book I came across this sentence: "In reality the so-called Franciscan virtues – poverty, humility, obedience, gratitude, holy joy, and genuine simplicity – do not stem from ascetic or moral zeal but from genuine "attentiveness" *(Aufmerksamkeit)* tied up with love for the Lord." Rohr uses the word "attentiveness" to translate a word which plays a role in all the descriptions of Francis and which is translated differently by different people. The Italian word, which Francis used, is "cortesia," which our dictionaries translate as "courtesy." But Romano Guardini had already drawn attention to the fact that *cortesia* meant much more to Francis than that. To him it meant the noble bearing of the knight, his kindly humaneness. And so we find Otto Karrer translating it variously as "knightly chivalry," "humaneness," "gentilezza," or "friendliness."

Joseph Bernhart, on the other hand, proposes "nobility" as the translation of "cortesia." He explains what it means: "It is not just the natural character of this man but the overall way in which he comprehended all reality, God and every being, and behaved towards them. Whatever virtue one may try to find in him, their common inspiration is his noble sense, his openheartedness to God and the world of men, to the highest and lowest being." Bernhart also says this:

"For Francis, religion is a relationship of noble to noble. It knows nothing of the meaner attitude of giving in order to get in return. The Lord is the good Lord: the Lord, but good; good, but the Lord.... The only fitting service to this Lord is service that wells up from a similar depth of nobility. Rendering this service is the affair of a spiritual and free creature, who should render it in the name of the lower creatures placed at his disposal as well. It is precisely this dignity of man's that obligates him to serve the honor of God. And this service, in turn, is the perfect fulfillment of his dignity.... We are only stewards, and the ultimate dignity of man lies in 'restoring' things to the Lord.... The love from above, which Francis at one point experienced by virtue of his natural and indeed prodigal capacity for love, was turned into the loving constraint of all those who had found the measure of love in loving without measure."

That is an erudite way of putting it. Francis expressed it much more simply. There is, for example, the story in the *Fioretti* that goes back to an actual event (as Karrer points out). One evening Francis and a companion came into the house of a rich and powerful nobleman, who received them with the greatest kindness *(con grandissima cortesia).* He embraced and kissed Francis as a friend, washed his feet, lit a cheerful fire, fed his guests well, and tended to them tirelessly with a cheerful countenance. He placed his riches at Francis' disposal. Francis had only to ask for whatever he needed, and this nobleman would foot the bill. When they took leave of him, Francis said to his companion:

"This kind man would be just right for our company. He is so thankful to God and has such *cortesia* for his fellow human beings and the poor. You know, dear Brother, such *cortesia* is an attribute of God. Out of *cortesia* he lavishes his sun and rain on the just and the unjust. *Cortesia* is a sister of charitableness, erasing hate and safeguarding love. Having seen such great and godly virtue in this man, I would gladly have him as a companion."

What does *cortesia* mean here? Is it decency, courtesy, nobleness, attentiveness, magnanimity, or knightliness?

I have used the French word *noblesse* as the title of this chapter. As far as I know, it does not appear in writings by or about Francis. Its meaning is related to the German word *Adel* (nobility) chosen by Joseph Bernhart to translate *cortesia* – except that it plays down the connotation of class standing, which also surfaces irritatingly in the words *cortesia, gentilezza,* and "knightliness." All these are expressions of a feudal age which we no longer know how to deal with at all. What is more, they are repugnant to us because we feel that the remnants of feudal thinking are one of the greatest obstacles on the pathway to a new age, especially in the Church. So we are led to reject all talk about *cortesia* out of hand, even in the case of Francis; it seems to be too bound up with a different age. In so doing, however, we are throwing the baby out with the bathwater. Of course Francis' language was tied to his own age. But the meaning which he gave to the word *cortesia,* and the basic attitude which lay behind it as he saw it, are things that go far beyond feudal thinking.

The word *noblesse* better expresses what Francis realized as *cortesia.* Perhaps we must go further and say that everything we designate today as *solidarity* with the suffering and the oppressed corresponds to the *cortesia* of Francis or, at the very least, does not run counter to it. I refer to real solidarity with those whose human dignity has been violated, so that we are prepared to share their lot and to fashion a community of disestablished people for the purpose of initiating effective action and bringing about structural change. But I do not want to equate solidarity completely with *cortesia.* For the latter signifies a very specific kind of solidarity that is essentially Christian in Francis' eyes.

The English word "gentleman" might well be brought up here, for it suggests a certain self-awareness. The gentleman knows his worth and does not give undue weight to what others say or think about him. Thus no one can insult him or get him angry. Desire for revenge is as alien to him as the jealousy which, in its countless witting and unwitting forms, poisons the world. Francis was such a gentleman through and through: always self-confident and self-possessed, never envious. The world "gentleman," however, does not give adequate expression to the social aspect. Indeed it bespeaks a certain cynicism towards human beings. For all his correctness, there is a certain lack of personal affection. The gentleman is always cool, and that certainly cannot be said of Francis. He was a social being through and through, oriented towards the "Thou" that others were.

This whole discussion of terminology may seem to be meaningless, but it actually leads us to a correct understanding of the *cortesia* of Francis. It contains much delicate reverence, but real involvement rather than standoffishness. It bespeaks a highly personal relationship, a concern for the person of one's fellow man. One's fellow man is valued objectively, but as a free person. His potential for good is recognized and appealed to, first and foremost; and his reprehensible traits are candidly and harshly described for what they are. Francis threatens people with the judgment of God astonishingly often. He warns people about the self-deception of the unrepentant sinner, of those who go to the sacraments mechanically without using their money for real social good. But such fulminations ever remain background phenomena. The main theme is awakening people to generosity — not to righteousness: for, Francis tells them that *cortesia* takes precedence over righteousness.

The most highly personal and existential affection for God and man, unconditional trust in them, a joyous appeal to their generosity: here lies the secret and the authentic merit of *cortesia* of Francis' invincible charm. Paul Sabatier, the great Protestant admirer of Francis, points out that there lies buried in the approach of the Poverello an ecumenical thrust, already alluded to in the Chronicle of Jordan of Giano. And in the Franciscan jubilee year of 1926, Friedrich Heiler wrote: "Shouldn't Francis be designated to win the world back to the Catholic ideal, even as he won back the divided Christians of the thirteenth century to church unity?"

I is Sabatier, the Huguenot scholar on Francis, who reminds us what wonders the poor man of Assisi worked in reconciling those separated from the universal Church in his day: "The *disputatores,* who were supposedly invincible, faded away before him. That, perhaps, is the most significant historical fact about the reformer from Assisi." Francis was stronger than they because he possessed the *noblesse* they lacked. With a sure instinct the common people sensed that a holy man was at work here — reforming the ancient Church, indeed, but in a different, a Christian, way.

And that brings us to the ultimate depths of the *cortesia,* the *noblesse,* of Francis of Assisi. In his classic statement about *cortesia* cited above, Francis says that "*cortesia* is a quality of God." It is not a chance observation. It characterizes the whole thought of Francis and shows what he thought being a Christian was. Two points stand out here, and both of them may be important for our own day.

The first has to do with his outlook on life and the world, his *Weltanschauung*. It would be a basic distortion to regard Francis as an early humanist; or to regard a global awareness of the unity of all men as the authentic root of his love of poverty; or to regard a dynamic thrust towards the future as the motor of his criticism of society. All these things can indeed be found in him. He loved human beings and had grand things to say about their dignity and freedom. He could also praise the wonder of the body, and there is no trace of prudery in him. But he possessed a *cosmic consciousness,* as the *Canticle of Brother Sun* shows. He calmly stepped beyond confessional and territorial boundaries, much to the dismay of the Order's Protector, who wanted to keep the friars in Italy. He is the first person from the West to wander through other continents in a peaceable and amiable way. He was aware of the unfolding development of man. And the kinship of his ideas with Joachim of Fiore's dynamic conception of history would excite those very friars who were dearest to him.

About all that there can be no doubt. But the greatest and most profound difference between his outlook and today's conceptions is that he related everything to one single reality, God. Even that statement is not correct, if we take it to mean that he moved from creatures up to God. That was not his approach. His approach was just the opposite: he started with God and saw all things from there. No one has put it as well as Chesterton:

"The transition from the good man to the saint is a sort of revolution; by which one for whom all things illustrate and illuminate God becomes one for whom God illustrates and illuminates all things. It is rather like the reversal whereby a lover might say at first sight that a lady looked like a flower, and say afterwards that all flowers reminded him of his lady. A saint and a poet standing by the same flower might seem to say the same thing; but indeed though they would both be telling the truth, they would be telling different truths. For one the joy of life is a *cause* of faith, for the other rather a *result* of faith. But one effect of the difference is that the sense of a divine dependence, which for the artist is like the brilliant levin-blaze, for the saint is like the broad daylight. Being in some mystical sense on the other

Pictures of the Umbrian landscape, pages 209–219:

THE CANTICLE OF BROTHER SUN

Most High, all-powerful, all good, Lord!
All praise is yours, all glory, all honor
And all blessing.
To you, alone, Most High, do they belong.
No mortal lips are worthy
To pronounce your name.

All praise be yours, my Lord, through all that you have made,
And first my lord Brother Sun,
Who brings the day; and light you give to us through him.
How beautiful is he, how radiant in all his splendor!
Of you, Most High, he bears the likeness.

All praise be yours, my Lord, through Sister Moon and Stars;
In the heavens you have made them, bright
And precious and fair.

All praise be yours, my Lord, through Brothers Wind and Air,
And fair and stormy, all the weather's moods,
By which you cherish all that you have made.

All praise be yours, my Lord, through Sister Water,
So useful, lowly, precious, and pure.

All praise be yours, my Lord, through Brother Fire,
Through whom you brighten up the night.
How beautiful is he, how gay! Full of power and strength.

All praise be yours, my Lord, through Sister Earth, our mother,
Who feeds us in her sovereignty and produces
Various fruits with colored flowers and herbs.

All praise be yours, my Lord, through those who grant pardon
For love of you; through those who endure
Sickness and trial.

Happy those who endure in peace,
By you, Most High, they will be crowned.

All praise be yours, my Lord, through Sister Death,
From whose embrace no mortal can escape.
Woe to those who die in mortal sin!
Happy those She finds doing your will!
The second death can do no harm to them.

Praise and bless my Lord, and give him thanks,
And serve him with great humility.

(Translation from B. Fahy and P. Hermann, *The Writings of St. Francis of Assisi*, Chicago, Ill.: Franciscan Herald Press, 1964, pp. 127–131.)

Picture page 220:
Rose-window of the basilica in Assisi. Built by Brother Elias of Cortona to honor Francis, it actually contradicts the truest heritage of his spirit. In it repose the remains of the saint.

side of things, he sees things go forth from the divine as children going forth from a familiar and accepted home, instead of meeting them as they come out, as most of us do, upon the roads of the world. And it is the paradox that by this privilege he is more familiar, more free and fraternal, more carelessly hospitable than we. For us the elements are like heralds who tell us with trumpet and tabard that we are drawing near the city of a great king; but he hails them with an old familiarity that is almost an old frivolity. He calls them Brother Fire and Sister Water" (Gilbert Chesterton, *St. Francis of Assisi,* New York: Doubleday Image Book, 1957, p. 76).

That is the *Weltanschauung* of Francis exactly. The present day could improve on that only by making it harder for us to see the approach of the poet. So we say that "God is dead," and we talk about the impossibility of encountering God in our self-sufficient world. Superficial as this observation may be, it still holds as a description of our awareness and living experience. That does not hold true for the other truth, which Chesterton describes as the truth of the saint. It holds now as before. All our new pieces of knowledge, put together, do not constrain the saint to change the smallest particle of his truth. On the contrary, they strengthen them.

What Francis saw and sought to incarnate, a bit ahead of his time, is now being confirmed today from the other side, so to speak. But we have lost one thing that constitutes the deepest core of all things: their personal value. For Francis, all things bore God's dedicated care for man. It is something immanent in all things; and the deeper man's mind probes into things, the better he can understand this dedication. That Francis thought so is indisputable: "God, who created us, is the best." He sees everything else by starting from God. That is how we must understand his association with nature too. He does not move from the gentleness of the lamb to God's goodness; on the contrary, he recalls the lamb in contemplating God's gentleness. He recalls the lark, his favorite bird, in contemplating God's gaiety. For him all things become the "mirror" of God. And because God is the creator of all things, they are his brothers and sisters. He does indeed personify God with them. But he never forgets that God is the best: "Without beginning and without end, he is unchangeable, invisible, indescribable and ineffable, incomprehensible, unfathomable, blessed and worthy of all praise, glorious, exalted, sublime, most high, kind, lovable, delightful and utterly desirable beyond all else, for ever and ever." Such talk about God is what we would call the *via negativa*. But he does not arrive at God by cooly calculating along this pathway. He came to God along the pathway of mysticism, through his inner experience of faith.

We may feel that Francis' experience of nature was quite superficial in this sense, and that there is much shoddy sentimentality in it. But was it really superficial? We may put his sermons to the birds into the category of legends, but legends are not just whimsical inventions. They embody an authentic assertion. In this case it is that animals felt instinctively drawn to Francis; that fact, supported by many stories, is undeniable. Animals felt sheltered and understood in his presence. That does not mean he was blind to the enigmatic abysses of nature, to its seeming contradictions and conflicts. He cursed a sow for gnawing a new-born lamb to death, even though the sow was God's creature too. He would release the fly and the drone from his hand, and yet he would address egotistical and worthless friars as "Brother Fly" and "Brother Drone." Why did this "sweet" saint like to withdraw to "wild and craggy landscapes" for weeks, so that he might plunge into contemplation of God? Because there he saw reflected the incomprehensibility and insolubility of it all. What seems to be shoddy sentimentality at first becomes astonishingly profound upon closer inspection. In the last analysis it is the divine likeness of things, their deepest core, which cannot be reached through scientific analysis. For analysts overlook this aspect of personal appeal.

I do not know whether this way – let us call it a mystical way – of encountering God is still a possible way for us today. When Karl Rahner suggests that we are approaching a mystagogic age in terms of experiencing God, he certainly has this in mind even though he may be thinking more about the meditation of Ignatius of Loyola on love at the end of his *Spiritual Exercises*. But the two saints are not really different on this point, for the meditation of Ignatius also points us towards finding God in all things.

But how did Francis manage to see all things from God? Only through faith, which is far more than an adherence to revealed truths. In his book on the mystery which grounds our life, Henri de Lubac, the man with the greatest *noblesse* among present-day theologians, has this to say:

"If we consider faith in terms of its full meaning, then it displays a host of essential features.... It is the firmest and surest of all the ways of knowing.... It is an essentially personal act, which engages existence at its deepest ground. It is an essentially religious act; indeed *the* religious act. To say faith is to say 'entrance into the realm of the hallowed.' The witness on which faith is grounded is the witness of God which does not, as human witness does, remain in an external relationship to the mind and spirit that receives it. God is not external to the being he has created. If indeed he is the 'Wholly Other,' he is not the 'Merely Other.' His voice resounds both outside and inside the one whom he calls to faith. Although faith may mean holding many things as truth... we can only speak of faith in the singular. Of its very nature faith is an answer to the revealing word of God which, insofar as it does reveal, reveals God. Our acceptance of things as true can apply to any human being. But our faith says that we believe our God and, in a deeper and more total way, move towards him. Our faith is our response to God's summons. That is more than an act of knowing; it is an act of acknowledgement: 'God, you have created us for yourself; we turn to you believingly and offer you our faith.'"

So we are back to our theme of *noblesse* again. For Francis, the quality which characterizes God in his dealings with men is *noblesse* and nothing else. It is not a system of ascesis that makes man perfect. It is not a universal love for man nor a series of moral precepts that are to be carried out faithfully and correctly. It is not the law of unfolding development or the idea of an ideal personality-image, according to which I am supposed to erect some static or dynamic monument to my self. No idea of an ideological cast dominates Francis' thought and action. His faith is his answer to the God who graciously reveals himself to him out of *noblesse*. And only one answer is possible on his part: *noblesse* in response to *noblesse.*

Therefore Francis' behavior towards God is not conscientious obedience. It is something more than the attitude which is so highly praised today: i. e., an objective stance towards some tenet. The latter is fully justified with respect to theoretical doctrine. But what is involved here is a message, a summons to respectful trust, a personal invitation to complete solidarity.

Out of this basic attitude towards God comes his *noblesse* towards his fellow men. Indeed it finds concrete expression in his fellow men, his brothers and sisters; and that means all human beings. Above all it means the poor, for they represent the strongest appeal to one's *noblesse* and are the mirror of God, who emptied himself out of *noblesse* in order to offer himself to the poor.

All this sheds light on our present day and its problems. The present age is very objective and very truth-oriented. It is singular in that respect. But in its reification of all things, persons, and even God, it overlooks the fact that there are personal values. Truth is Person, and there is no fact or idea that is not deeply marked by a personal value. When Francis was to be treated for his eye trouble, the procedure, entailing the use of a hot iron, was very painful; for the use uf narcotics was unknown. Francis said to the fire: "My Brother Fire, you are noble and useful among God's creatures. Now be noble *(cortese)* to me. I have always loved you, and I will ever do so for the sake of him who created you. I implore our Creator to deign to cool your heat, so that I can bear it!"

For Francis all creation was a gesture of *noblesse* towards man by God. For us it is an object of research, and a tool that man uses to fashion a better humanity. The two attitudes do not rule each other out. But we have forgotten the attitude of the Poverello today in our exaltation over our new dominion, and as a result we have fallen prey to anxiety. With Francis we could free ourselves from this anxiety and transform it into hope. When the doctor was treating Francis for his eye trouble, he was astonished to see how calm and cool Francis remained. And when the hot-iron treatment was over, Francis said to his friars: "You of little heart, why did you run away when they were burning me? I will tell you quite honestly, I felt no pain at all!"

The Last Words Spoken by Francis of Assisi

Psalm 142 (141)

I cry with my voice to the Lord,
With my voice I make supplication to the Lord,
I pour out my complaint before him,
I tell my trouble before him.
When my spirit is faint,
Thou knowest my way!

In the path where I walk
They have hidden a trap for me.
I look to the right and watch,
But there is none who takes notice of me;
No refuge remains to me,
No man cares for me.

I cry to thee, O Lord,
I say, Thou art my refuge,
My portion in the land of the living.
Give heed to my cry;
For I am brought very low!

Deliver me from my persecutors;
For they are too strong for me!
Bring me out of prison,
That I may give thanks to thy name!
The righteous will surround me;
For thou wilt deal bountifully with me.

(Translation from the Revised Standard Version.)

7. Chronology

Note: The prototypes for the illustrations in this Chronology were provided by the picture archives of the Berlin Staatsbibliothek, the Archives for History and the Fine Arts in Berlin, and the picture archives of the publisher, C. J. Bucher.

In a dream Pope Innocent III sees the collapsing church being saved by Francis of Assisi; detail from the Assisi-frescoes by Giotto.

EVENTS IN THE LIFE
OF ST. FRANCIS

1181/ Francis is born in Assisi, the
1182 son of the wealthy merchant, Pietro Bernardone. He is christened Giovanni, but called Francesco by his father who often traveled to France on business and had a special liking for that country.

*Francis of Assisi;
fresco by Cimabue.*

EVENTS IN CONTEMPORARY
HISTORY

1183 In Constance, Emperor Frederick I Barbarossa enters an alliance with the Lombard cities. The Emperor is recognized as feudal lord.

1184 Discussions between the Emperor and the Pope in Verona about heresy in Northern Italy.
Betrothal of the Emperor's son, Henry VI, and Constance of Sicily.

1185 Pope Urban (1185–1187), a bitter enemy of the Emperor. He never resided in Rome.

1187 Pope Gregory VIII. Agreement made with the Emperor.
Pope Clement III (1187–1191). Returns to Rome and is acknowledged by the Romans where the Senate had ruled since 1144.

1189 Beginning of the Third Crusade under the leadership of Frederick Barbarossa.

1190 Barbarossa drowns in Seleí River (Asia Minor). He is succeeded by Henry VI (1190–1197).

1191 Pope Celestine III (1191–1198).
Henry VI crowned Emperor by Celestine. Richard the Lionheart taken into custody by the Emperor during his return from the Crusade; conciliates the Guelphs and becomes vassal of the Emperor.

	1194 Henry VI takes Sicily. Coronation in Palermo as King of Sicily. Birth of Frederick II. Celestine decides to resign.
	1197 Henry VI dies before the realization of his plan to create a hereditary kingdom.
1198 Conrad, Count of Assisi, is driven out and his castle razed. Democratic *popolani* seize power. Two consuls hold top post.	1198 Pope Innocent III (1198–1216). The Senators of Rome resign. The Pope becomes guardian of Frederick II. In Germany the fateful double election of both King Philip of Swabia (1189–1208) and Otto IV of Brunswick (1198–1215), nephew of Richard the Lionheart. The imperial power begins to disintegrate.
1202 Francis takes part in the war of Assisi against Perugia, a Ghibelline city; he spends a year in prison and returns home sick.	1202 Death of Joachim of Fiore. Beginning of the Fourth Crusade.
1205 Francis' outlook begins to change. He seeks to join the papal forces of Walter de Brienne. His plan falls apart at Apulia.	1203 Fall of Constantinople; the plundering of the city against the wishes of the Pope. Erection of a Latin kingdom (1204–1261).
1206 First visit to Rome. Tries out being a beggar. Hears a voice from the Cross in San Damiano: "Rebuild my house."	
1207 Break with his father — period of wandering. He restores churches and chapels: San Damiano, Portiuncula, etc.	1208 Philip of Swabia murdered in Bamberg. Otto IV the sole ruler. Frederick II, fourteen years old, takes over the government of Sicily.

1209*	Decisive experience in Portiuncula upon hearing the gospel of the Mass (Matthew 10, 7–20).
1210*	First approval of Friars Minor (Ordinis Fratrum Minorum – OFM). Francis receives the tonsure. "Magna Charta" of Assisi: agreement between upper and lower classes.
1211	The Benedictines let Francis have the chapel of Portiuncula.
1212	On March 18 Clare joins Francis.
1213	Attempt to go to the Holy Land.
1215	Fourth Lateran Council. Francis meets Dominic.

* The commonly accepted dates are 1208 and 1209 (not 1209 and 1210). See Chronology in *St. Francis of Assisi, First and Second Life of St. Francis . . .* by *Thomas of Celano*, trans. by P. Hermann (Chicago: Franciscan Herald Press, 1962), p. 216; paperback edn., p. 328.

1209	King Otto IV marches to Rome where he is crowned Emperor by Innocent. Beginning of the Albigensian War in Southern France – often called the Albigensian Crusade (1209–1229).
1210	Emperor Otto IV excommunicated because he, taking up the policy of the Hohenstaufens, had decided to take control of Sicily.
1211	Diet of Nürnberg: Frederick II elected German anti-king (alongside Otto IV).
1212	Frederick II (1212–1250).
1214	Otto IV decisively beaten by French King Philip Augustus II. He dies alone in 1218.
1215	Fourth Lateran Council. Innocent says that all evil stems from the clergy. In England the barons force King John I (John Lackland) to sign the Magna Charta. It forms the foundation of every future constitution.

Mary with the Child Jesus; before her, Francis of Assisi in his capacity as the founder of an Order. Painting by Benozzo Gozzoli (section).

Francis presents the rule of his Order to Pope Honorius III; fresco by Giotto in Santa Croce, Florence.

1216	First meeting with Ugolino of Ostia, later Pope Gregory IX, in Perugia. Portiuncula indulgence requested from Pope Honorius III (?).	1216	Pope Honorius III (1216–1227).
1217	Pentecost chapter: friars sent out on mission to the whole world.	1217/ 1218	Crusade under King Andrew II of Hungary.
1218	Sermon before the Pope and Cardinals about the vices of the Curia. Ugolino becomes the Protector of the Friars Minor at the request of Francis.		
1219	Francis in Egypt with the crusaders; visits the Sultan.	1219	November: crusaders capture Damietta in the Nile delta.
1221	Second version of the Rule worked out with Caesar of Speyer; debated on May 30 at the Chapter of Mats. In a speech Francis opposes accommodation to old Orders.	1220	Frederick II crowned Emperor in Rome.
		1221	Defeat and withdrawal of the crusaders.

1222 Third version of the Rule "lost" by Brother Elias.
1223 Fourth version of the Rule debated at General Chapter on June 11.
Francis resigns leadership of the Order.
Elias Bombarone (Elias of Cortona) becomes Vicar General.
Pope Honorius solemnly approves this Rule in November — therefore known as the *(regula) bullata*.
1224 Letter to all Christians. Francis at Mount La Verna; receives the stigmata on September 17.
1225 Francis stays at San Damiano near Clare, composes the first part "The Canticle of Brother Sun." Undergoes eye operation in Rieti, returns to Assisi and adds two verses.
1226 Francis dies on October 3, immediately after singing Psalm 142 (141).

1228 Francis of Assisi canonized by Gregory IX on July 15.

1230 Transfer of the remains of St. Francis to the patriarchal basilica of Assisi.

Clare of Assisi;
fresco by Simone Martini in Assisi.

1226 Louis IX, St. Louis, becomes King of France.
1227 Cardinal Ugolino becomes Pope Gregory IX.
Emperor Frederick II excommunicated because he delays leading a crusade as he had promised.
1228/ Fifth Crusade under the leadership of the excommunicated Frederick. In 1229 he obtained the holy cities of Nazareth, Bethlehem, and Jerusalem by a treaty with the Egyptian Sultan.
1229
1230 Treaty of San Germano: Frederick II submits to Gregory IX and excommunication is lifted.

8. Bibliography

This bibliography, prepared by the editor, lists selected English titles on the sources of the life of St. Francis, biographies, works on his message, his spirit, and his Orders. For more complete bibliographies see Masseron-Habig, *The Franciscans,* pp. 479–506, and Englebert, *St. Francis of Assisi,* pp. 497–601. An omnibus of all the early lives of St. Francis and other sources is in preparation and will be published by Franciscan Herald Press, Chicago (abbreviated FHP).

Quotations of the Bible are from the *Revised Standard Version* (New York: Oxford University Press, 1965); of the documents of Vatican II, from W. M. Abbott, ed., *The Documents of Vatican II* (New York: Angelus Book, 1966).

SOURCES

BROOKE, ROSALIND B. *Scripta Leonis, Rufini et Angeli, Sociorum S. Francisci: The Writings of Leo, Rufino and Angelo, Companions of St. Francis.* Oxford: Clarendon, 1970.

BROWN, RAPHAEL, trans., ed. *Fifty Animal Stories of Saint Francis as Told by His Companions.* Chicago: FHP, 1958.
The Little Flowers of St. Francis. Garden City, N. Y.: Hannover, 1958.
Our Lady and Saint Francis: All the Earliest Texts. Chicago: FHP, 1954.

FAHY BENEN, trans., and PLACID HERMANN, ed. *The Writings of St. Francis.* Chicago: FHP, 1964.

HERMANN, PLACID, trans., ed. *St. Francis of Assisi: First and Second Life of St. Francis, with Selections from Treatise on the Miracles of Blessed Francis, by Thomas of Celano.* Chicago: FHP, 1962.
Via Seraphica: Selected Readings from the Early Documents and Writings Pertaining to St. Francis and the Franciscan Order. Chicago: FHP, 1959.

KARRER, OTTO, ed. *St. Francis of Assisi: The Legends and Lauds,* trans. by N. Wydenbruck. London and New York, 1948.

MASSERON, ALEXANDRE, ed. *Memorable Words of Saint Francis,* trans. by Margaret Sullivan. Chicago: FHP, 1963.

MEYER, JAMES, trans., ed. *The Words of St. Francis: An Anthology.* Chicago: FHP, 1952, 1966.

ROBECK, NESTA DE, and PLACID HERMANN. *St. Francis of Assisi: His Holy Life and Love of Poverty (Legend of the Three Companions,* trans. by

N. de Robeck, and *Sacrum Commercium*, trans. by P. Hermann). Chicago: FHP, 1964.

ROGGEN, HERIBERT, trans., ed. *Spirit and Life: The Gospel Way of Life in the Writings of St. Francis and St. Clare.* Chicago: FHP, 1970.

SHIRLEY PRICE, LEO, trans., ed. *St. Francis of Assisi: His Life and Writings as Recorded by His Contemporaries* (the life is *Speculum Perfectionis*). New York: Harcourt, 1959.

VIAN NELLO, ed. *Golden Words: The Sayings of Brother Giles of Assisi*, trans. by Ivo O'Sullivan. Chicago: FHP, 1966.

BIOGRAPHIES

ANCELET-HUSTACHE, JEANNE. *Once Upon a Time in Assisi: The Life of Saint Francis Told to Children*, trans. by Sister M. Clarissa. Chicago: FHP, 1955.

CHESTERTON, GILBERT. *St. Francis of Assisi.* New York: Doubleday Image Books, 1957.

CUTHBERT, FATHER. *Life of St. Francis of Assisi.* Third edition. London and New York: Longmans, 1912–1960.

ENGLEBERT, OMER. *St. Francis of Assisi: A Biography,* trans. by Eve Marie Cooper, revised and augmented by Ignatius Brady and Raphael Brown. Chicago: FHP, 1965.

HEGENER, MARK. *The Poverello: St. Francis of Assisi.* Chicago: FHP, 1956.

HERMANN, PLACID. *Seraph of Love* (life of St. Francis in blank verse). Chicago: FHP, 1959.

JÖRGENSEN, JOHANNES. *St. Francis of Assisi: A Biography,* trans. by T. O'Conor Sloane. London and New York, 1912; Garden City, N. Y., 1955.

LLOYD, TERESA. *The Poor Man of Assisi: Saint Francis.* Chicago: FHP, 1962.

HERITAGE

AEBY, GERVAIS, et al. *Call to Commitment: In the School of St. Francis,* trans. by Michael D. Meilach. Chicago: FHP, 1964.

BETTONI, EFREM. *Nothing for Your Journey,* trans. by Bruce Malina. Chicago: FHP, 1959.

BRADY, IGNATIUS, trans., ed. *The Marrow of the Gospel: A Study of the Rule of Saint Francis of Assisi by the Franciscans of Germany.* Chicago: FHP, 1958.

BRETON, VALENTINE-M. *Franciscan Spirituality,* trans. by Flavian Frey. Chicago: FHP, 1957.
In Christ's Company, trans. by Michael D. Meilach. Chicago: FHP, 1961.
Lady Poverty, trans. by Paul J. Oligny. Chicago: FHP, 1963.

CORSTANJE, AUSPICIUS VAN. *The Covenant with God's Poor: A Biblical Interpretation of the Testament of St. Francis.* Chicago: FHP, 1966.

CROSBY, JEREMIAH. *Bearing Witness: The Place of the Franciscan Family in the Church.* Chicago: FHP, 1966.

DUKKER, CHRYSOSTOMUS. *The Changing Heart: The Penance Concept of St. Francis of Assisi,* trans. by Bruce Malina. Chicago: FHP, 1963.

ENGEMANN, ANTONELLUS. *The New Song: Faith, Hope, and Charity in Franciscan Spirituality,* trans. by Isabel and Florence McHugh. Chicago: FHP, 1964.

ESSER, CAJETAN. *The Order of St. Francis: Its Spirit and Its Mission in the Kingdom of God,* trans. by Ignatius Brady. Chicago: FHP, 1959.
Origins of the Franciscan Order, trans. by Aedan Daly and Irina Lynch. Chicago: FHP, 1970.
Repair My House, ed. by Luc Mely, trans. by Michael D. Meilach. Chicago: FHP, 1963.
and ENGELBERT GRAU. *Love's Reply,* trans. by Ingnatius Brady. Chicago: FHP, 1963.

EUGENE, CHRISTIAN. *Our Lady: Devotion to Mary in Franciscan Tradition.* Chicago: FHP, 1954.

FELDER, HILARIN. *The Ideals of St. Francis of Assisi,* trans. by Berchmans Bittle. New York: Benziger, 1925.

GEMELLI, AGOSTINO. *Franciscan Message to the World (Il francescanesimo).* London: Burns Oates and Washbourne, 1934.
The Message of St. Francis, trans. by Paul J. Oligny. Chicago: FHP, 1963.

HABIG, MARION A. *The Franciscan Book of Saints.* Chicago: FHP, 1959.
New Catechism of the Third Order. Revised edition. Chicago: FHP, 1967.
Franciscan Pictorial Book. Chicago: FHP, 1963.
and ALBERT J. NIMETH. *Franciscan Pictorial Book Two.* Chicago: FHP, 1966.

HALLACK, CECILY, and PETER F. ANSON. *These Made Peace: Studies in the Lives of the Beatified and Canonized Members of the Third Order of St. Francis of Assisi,* ed. by Marion A. Habig. London: Burns and Oates; Paterson, N. J.: St. Anthony Guild Press, 1957.

HANSON, WARREN G. *St. Francis of Assisi: Patron of Environment.* Chicago, FHP, 1971.

HEGENER, MARK, ed. *The Franciscan Vision of Life: The Address "Nel Darvi" of Pope Pius XII with Articles Explaining the Franciscan Way of Living.* Chicago: FHP, 1957.
and MARION A. HABIG. *A Short History of the Third Order.* Chicago: FHP, 1963.

HERMANN, PLACID. *The Way of St. Francis.* Chicago: FHP, 1964.

KANN, SR. JEAN M. *I Found Francis in Assisi.* Chicago: FHP, 1960.

LECLERC, ELOI. *Wisdom of the Poverello,* trans. by Marie Louise Johnson. Chicago: FHP, 1961.

LEKEUX, MARTIAL. *Twentieth Century Litany to the Poverello.* Chicago: FHP, 1958.

MASSERON, ALEXANDRE, and MARION A. HABIG. *The Franciscans: St. Francis of Assisi and His Three Orders*. Chicago: FHP, 1959.

LONGPRÉ, EFREM. *A Poor Man's Peace* (the spirit of St. Francis), trans. by Paul Barrett. Chicago: FHP, 1968.

MEYER, JAMES. *A Primer of Perfection for Everybody*. Chicago: FHP, 1946. *Social Ideals of St. Francis: Eight Lessons in Applied Christianity*. Second revised edition. St. Louis and London: B. Herder, 1948.

MOORMAN, JOHN. *A History of the Franciscan Order from Its Origins to the Year 1517*. Oxford: Clarendon, 1968.

MOREAU, ABEL. *On Leave from Heaven*, trans. by Flavian Frey. Chicago: FHP, 1955.

MOTTE, JOHN FRANCIS. *Face to the World: The Third Order in Modern Society*, trans. by Margaret Sullivan. Chicago: FHP, 1960.

NIMETH, ALBERT J. *There is More to Life than Living It: The Third Order Rule as Practical Christianity*. Chicago: FHP, 1955.

O'ROURKE, DANIEL. *How to Live in a Layman's Order*. Chicago: FHP, 1964.

PIAT, STEPHANE J. *How to Be an Instrument of Peace: The Message of Saint Francis to the World*, trans. by Paul J. Oligny and Barnabas Abel. Chicago: FHP, 1955.

Riches and the Spirit, trans. by Paul J. Oligny. Chicago: FHP, 1958.

PIDOUX DE LA MADUERE, SYLVAIN. *Our Brother the Death of the Body*, trans. by James Meyer. Chicago: FHP, 1947.

POPE LEO XIII and Successors. *Rome Hath Spoken* (papal encyclicals on the Third Order of St. Francis), trans. by James Meyer. Chicago: FHP, 1943.

SCHNEIDER, REINHOLD. *The Hour of Saint Francis of Assisi*, trans. by James Meyer. Chicago, FHP, 1953.

WROBLEWSKI, SERGIUS. *Christian Perfection for the Layman*. Chicago: FHP, 1963.